D0422146

CHANGES IN WORKING TIME

AN INTERNATIONAL REVIEW

PAUL BLYTON

ST. MARTIN'S PRESS
New York

Library of Congress Cataloging in Publication Data

Main entry under title:
Blyton, Paul.
   Changes in working time.

   Bibliography: p.
   Includes indexes.
   1. Hours of labor.   I. Title.
HD5106.B59   1985   331.25′7   85-14562
ISBN 0-312-12937-8

CONTENTS

FIGURES

TABLES

Tables

PREFACE

For some time prior to writing this book, I had been interested in the work-sharing argument and the possibilities for modifying working time as a basis of creating additional employment. The more I became involved with this idea, however, the more I grew conscious that this was only one of a number of issues challenging the logic of existing worktime patterns. In the same way as a high and sustained level of unemployment questioned the efficacy and equity of the current structure of working time, so too did the interests of women and older workers and those involved in manual occupations. Moreover, the fundamental changes to work organization being instigated by new technology represent another potential source of challenge to the worktime structure. A key common question appeared to be whether working time was capable of offering a greater degree of variation, choice and flexibility than had been typical hitherto — flexibility to meet changing societal, as well as individual and organizational, needs. It is with this general question in mind that I have sought to review the main developments taking place within different aspects of working time.

In acknowledging the help I have enjoyed whilst writing this book, I would like to mention particularly my wife, Ticky, who has borne with patience the detritus of manuscript preparation that has spread gradually throughout our home; my nextdoor neighbour, Gordon, who not only gave me the benefit of his wisdom over the garden hedge, but also kept the hedge cut whilst I stayed inside pretending to work; and Kath Hollister for her patience in typing and retyping and especially for her Valleys good humour.

1 INTRODUCTION

In the eighteenth century, the combination of technical innovations that we know as the Industrial Revolution made the factory both feasible and dominant. From the 1770s on, then, an increasing number of workers found themselves employed at jobs that required them to appear by a set time every morning and work a day whose duration and wage were a function of the clock.

Nothing was harder. These were people who were accustomed to work at their own pace to take their rest, and distraction, or for that matter relieve themselves, as and when they pleased . . . Coming as they did from cottages and fields they felt the factory to be a kind of jail, with the clock as the lock (Landes, 1983, p. 229).

In all these ways — by the division of labour; the supervision of labour; fines; bells and clocks; money incentives; preachings and schoolings; the suppression of fairs and sports — new labour habits were formed and a new time-discipline imposed (Thompson, 1967, p. 90).

For Landes and Thompson, the Industrial Revolution marks a fundamental change in the significance of time in the work process. Time discipline, time keeping, the control of time — these became key characteristics of an industrial system based on predictability, regularity, synchronization of production and maximization of output. Two centuries away from the Industrial Revolution time remains a principal component of the modern work organization and a crucial aspect of the bargain struck between employer and worker. Start and stop times, overtime, part-time, 'flexitime', time and motion — time represents an essential characteristic of the nature and experience of work. The organization and control of time remain central to the organization and control of work and the work organization.

Yet, whilst the importance of time in the work-place has remained — not to say strengthened by the various technological

1

changes which have occurred — the actual patterns of worktime have undergone considerable modification, a number of these changes being most evident in the last two decades.

The aim of this book is to identify the ways working time has developed in recent years, evaluating the significance of the changes and highlighting the major factors which have influenced both change and stability in working time patterns. A central purpose of this endeavour is to achieve a capability to evaluate the various arguments which currently challenge the logic of existing worktime arrangements. Such an enquiry would seem to be overdue. Despite the changes which have occurred, and the significance of working time not only for other aspects of work but also for wider spheres of family and community life, this feature of work organization has not attracted the range of investigation it deserves. Moreover, much of the previous research directed towards working time (as distinct from the many studies of work which have indirectly shed light on aspects of worktime) has considered single facets of the worktime pattern, such as overtime, shiftwork, compressed schedules or retirement. Whilst this work has been valuable, so too is the wider approach which seeks to take in the various developments occurring in individual aspects, in search of a more general understanding of the broader trends and possibilities for future worktime patterns. Given the nature of questions confronting the present configuration of working time — in general, its appropriateness in the context of profound changes in economic, social and technological circumstances — this broader approach appears to offer considerable potential reward even if, regrettably, at times this has to be at the cost of a less than comprehensive investigation of issues surrounding any one particular feature of working time.

What is the nature of this challenge to the existing pattern of working time? What are the arguments for change, and what changes are sought? It is with these questions, together with an outline of subsequent chapters, that the remainder of the introduction is concerned.

Arguments for Change

More than at any other time this century the logic of existing worktime patterns is being questioned. The sources of this challenge are many and varied, reflecting not only the breadth of the subject (e.g. ranging from questions of school-leaving age to those of retirement, and from optimum length of shifts to the benefits of sabbatical leave) but also the interrelation of working time and other aspects of the social system, such as marriage, child-rearing, education and community activity. Whilst the sources of criticism of existing patterns vary, one theme common to several concerns the call for a greater degree of choice and flexibility in working time arrangements, so as to reflect the growing diversity of the contemporary workforce, the varied needs of different groups, the different technologies being applied and the different economic outlook from that prevailing in previous decades. Later chapters will examine the scope for change in this direction, partly by examining the diversity and flexibility which has already developed in worktime patterns in Britain and abroad; but first let us turn briefly to some of the main arguments for change.

The Work-sharing Argument

During previous periods of high unemployment, it has been common for workers' representatives to call for a cut in working hours and a more even distribution of jobs among the working population as a whole. Often quoted, for example, is Samuel Gompers, the American trade union leader who in 1887 commented that 'As long as we have one person seeking work who cannot find it, the hours of work are too long' (quoted in MaCoy and Morand, 1984). Contemporary examples can also be found in the annals of British labour history, notably in the campaign for an eight hour day in the 1880s and 1890s (Harris, 1972). Almost a century later in the late 1970s and 1980s, the high and sustained level of unemployment has similarly given rise to calls for worksharing, with trade union organizations and others calling for reductions in working time as one measure to counter the shortage of jobs. Within individual countries this general call has been translated into various specific demands for change in the pattern of worktime, including the introduction of a shorter working week, longer holidays, reductions in overtime working and greater provision for early retirement (Blyton, 1982a).

In this latest period, the work-sharing argument has been reinforced by future projections of unemployment which suggest that in most Western industrialized countries, unemployment is likely to remain at or above its present high level for the foreseeable future,[1] unless far greater efforts towards its alleviation are made, than have been attempted hitherto. In part this pessimistic prediction reflects the multi-causal nature of unemployment, which includes not only domestic and international recession and responding deflationary policies, but also the transformation of formerly labour-intensive manufacturing industries, a growth in the size of labour forces (partly reflecting changing attitudes among married women towards work), increasing competition from newly industrializing countries, and the potential labour-saving capacity of those advances and innovations which come under the umbrella title of 'new technology'.

The argument for a reduction and redistribution of working time has not gone uncriticized, however. Employers and various governments, both in Britain and abroad, have criticized work-sharing principally on the grounds that if this reduction in hours were not accompanied by a fall in earnings (a position being sought by most trade unions), then the resulting increase in labour costs would damage competitiveness in such a way as to bring about a loss in sales and an overall *increase* in unemployment, rather than the intended opposite (Confederation of British Industry, 1980; Department of Employment, 1978b).

These claims and counter-claims for work-sharing remain unresolved, partly because of the sweeping generalizations made on both sides. What is required is a more careful appraisal of the proposals in the light of working time changes already occurring, including work-sharing initiatives introduced in individual countries in recent years. In conjunction with knowledge of people's preferences for different worktime arrangements, and a more disaggregated approach to the work-sharing arguments, greater insight is possible into the conditions under which work-sharing could be both cost effective and job creative. This is one of the tasks undertaken in Chapter 2.

The Discretion/Choice Argument

In the past two decades, the concept of workers' participation in decision-making has received widespread attention both from management and unions. On the one hand, management have fostered 'motivational' forms of participation which involve little sharing of real decision-making powers and have as their main goal increases in worker commitment and productivity (the emphasis of these forms is on 'involvement' rather than shared influence).

Trade unions, on the other hand, have focused their aspirations much more on 'power-sharing' forms of participation, in which the influence sharing through joint decision-making bodies is more explicit and the objective a democratization of the workplace. The development of both types of participation machinery has been far from uniform; indeed, some writers have argued that the development of workers' participation has been cyclical in nature, growing during periods of labour shortage but decaying in times of weak labour power (Ramsay, 1977). Given certain factors, however, such as the legislative underpinning of participation in some countries, and possibly changes in employee expectations and attitudes to traditional patterns of authority and subordination, it is arguable that the cycles of participation have in fact been situated on a rising trend, such that over a long period of time the extent of employee participation in workplace decision-making has been increasing, albeit slowly.

One aspect of work which has yielded very little to increased employee influence, however, is the pattern of working time. Any increase in worker control which participation has engendered has been concentrated on such issues as the organization of the work task and aspects of working conditions, and not on the pattern of working time. Indeed, whilst various aspects of the structure and process of the work organization have been subject to considerable change, a number of the features of worktime patterns have exhibited a high degree of institutional rigidity. Of course, increased discretion and participation in working time decisions has not been completely absent; the growth in 'flexitime' arrangements among (mainly white-collar) workgroups, for example, has been one way in which the degree of choice has been extended. In other areas, however, such as the ability to choose one's age and rate of retirement, or the flexibility to transfer from full-time to part-time working (and vice versa), the amount of discretion available has remained, for the most part, highly restricted.

The extent to which changes occurring in recent years represent a significant increase in flexibility, the indication of patterns of preference among workforces for different worktime arrangements, and the evidence of employers' ability to incorporate successfully a greater degree of freedom over working time, are important issues which crop up at several points throughout the book.

The Argument Relating to Changes in the Labour Force

It may be argued that the predominance of jobs which take up around eight hours a day for five days a week for 46 to 48 weeks a year, is a pattern most appropriate to a society typified by family organization where one of the adults (usually the male) is engaged in outside employment, whilst the other takes responsibility for housekeeping and child-rearing activities. Yet, as has been well documented, recent years have witnessed a considerable change in the overall pattern of the labour force, and in particular the marked rise in the employment of married women (Clark, 1982; Dex and Perry, 1984). The reasons for this are several, and include rising material expectations, changes in female (and male) attitudes to paid employment, the changing demand for labour due to the expansion of the service sector, and the trend towards smaller families which has helped to reduce the overall length of time that women are involved in child-rearing.

Many of the jobs held by married women are part-time. Yet despite the growing importance of part-time work (in Britain, approximately 20 per cent of all jobs are part-time, and among women workers 42 per cent of jobs in 1981 were part-time), in many ways the availability of part-time work has remained highly circumscribed. This is reflected not only in the low levels of pay, status, security and promotion prospects which typify most part-time jobs, but also in the general lack of opportunities available for switching from full-time to part-time employment. The growing support for job-sharing, whereby two people share the responsibilities of one full-time job, represents one attempt to overcome some of the traditional limitations of part-time working by creating access to better paid and more challenging part-time jobs. Yet, in the short term at least, the widespread diffusion of the job-sharing concept faces a number of major obstacles; these, together with the extent to which this innovation in working time has managed to establish a foothold in different countries and the other developments occurring in part-time working, are examined in Chapter 6.

The Equality/Harmonization Argument

A greater number of advantages continue to be associated with being a non-manual/white-collar, rather than a manual/blue-collar, worker. Managerial and other white-collar employees 'on the staff' have traditionally enjoyed shorter hours than their manual counterparts, longer holidays and less shift-working, as well as better pay, improved sickness benefits, pension entitlement and better canteen facilities — the list covers virtually all aspects of the terms, conditions and environment of work. Together with the unequal treatment of men and women in employment (particularly with respect to access to higher grade jobs), this differential treatment of blue-collar and white-collar workers continues to represent a major source of inequality in industry (Littler and Salaman, 1984).

Yet even in Britain, where the more prominent class system may have exacerbated the clear drawing of distinctions between manual and non-manual workers, some reductions in inequality have taken place in recent years. In working-time aspects, for example, differences in holiday entitlement have been reduced and the variation in weekly hours somewhat diminished. Yet considerable differences in treatment still remain. In Britain in 1984, the average full-time male manual worker worked over 44 hours per week (including overtime) whereas his white-collar counterpart worked around 38½ hours; over a working lifetime of 40 years, this means that the blue-collar worker is working the hours equivalent of *more than five years longer* than the white-collar worker,[2] and in conditions which are generally far more unsafe, unhealthy and typically less personally fulfilling and financially rewarding.

With the routinization of many white-collar tasks (and the associated reduction in education needed for, and status attached to, those jobs), together with the proliferation both of white-collar employment and those on the margin of the blue-collar/white-collar distinction (various types of technical jobs, operators of computer-controlled machines, etc.), this difference in treatment is becoming even more difficult to justify or sustain than previously. The call by representatives of manual workers to harmonize the working time patterns of blue- and white-collar grades may be expected to be a major focus of parity arguments in coming years.

The Technology and Organizational Efficiency Argument

Most Western industrialized societies have been witnessing fundamental changes occurring both in their industrial structures and within individual workplaces. At the general level, the main changes taking place have involved the long-term transformation of a number of primary and manufacturing industries, in particular the large-scale de-manning of such industries as coal-mining, iron and steel production, dock-working and ship-building. In the 1970s this was accompanied by a substantial growth in service industries, to a point where in several countries a majority of workers are now employed in the service sector, which covers such disparate activities as local and central government, education, health, banking and insurance, the tourist and entertainment industries and retailing.

In parallel with these macro-level changes have been significant developments within the workplace, in particular the application of new electronic technologies, both in the office (microcomputers, word processors, text transfer equipment, etc.) and increasingly on the shop-floor (computer numerical control machines, robotics, etc.). A widening range of jobs from paint-spraying to typing, tool-making to record-keeping are being rapidly transformed by the flexibility of the integrated circuit and the modern computer.

Given this scale of change in the way work is carried out, it is not surprising that pre-existing patterns of working time are beginning to be called more into question as to their suitability for the contemporary society. The length of the working week, the current organization of shift-working, established patterns of overtime, and the ratio of full-time to part-time employment, may each be seen to be increasingly problematic in the light of the technological and structural changes taking place. In addition, other working time aspects may soon be demanding attention as a result of technological change. One of these, which has so far attracted more media interest than actual introduction, is the question of whether certain types of non-manual work actually requires employees to travel to their traditional workplace five times each week, or whether some of the work can be done from home by being linked to the office by computer terminal.

Broader Societal Arguments

As the final decade of the twentieth century nears, it is appropriate to ask broader questions about the suitability of current working time patterns. Certain specific issues have already been raised. In the field of transportation and urban planning, for example, the advantages of staggering work times and/or reducing the total numbers of journeys in order to minimize time spent in congested travel, have been discussed (see Chapter 7). Other no less important social questions have received less attention, however — for example, the implications of increased average life expectancy both for retirement policy and for the continued fixed nature of the education–work–retirement sequence. More generally, an important element in the overall quality of life is the extent to which the different social institutions in which individuals participate — work, family, education, etc. — mesh satisfactorily together. Clearly, the time pattern of work exerts a strong influence on the scope for performing other social activities such as child-rearing, acquiring further education, pursuing leisure interests, or fulfilling different community roles. One of the general questions to be posed, therefore, is whether existing worktime patterns allow an equilibrium to be created between work and non-work activities. Any analysis of developments in working time cannot afford to overlook the broader associations between work and society.

A Word on Obstacles to Change

As forthcoming chapters will demonstrate, a number of changes are occurring in working time patterns which, taken together, appear to represent both a significant development in the nature of work organization, and indication of possible changes to come. Yet it is also important at the outset to note that some aspects of working time have been extraordinarily resistant to change. Most working people continue to be faced with a rigid and institutional-ized working time structure, offering few opportunities for exercising choice and discretion over their pattern of working time. Resistance to certain changes by management may emanate from a number of sources, not least the potential for calls for greater flexi-bility to run counter to managerial objectives of increasing control and co-ordination over the labour input. Other obstacles are also likely to include 'objective' factors — for example the problem of reconciling a round-the-clock shift system with a 35 hour working week — as well as 'subjective' ones, such as management per-ceiving greater working time choice as creating administrative problems. Many obstacles to and criticisms of change are high-lighted at different points in the book. Here it is sufficient to note that though the changes identified may represent the beginnings of a major shift in the pattern of worktime arrangements, their further development is not automatically assured but, on the contrary, is likely to meet with considerable resistance from different quarters; hence the need for an examination and evalua-tion of the developments to date.

Outline of the Book

The most important changes in working time are occuring not in a single country but in a variety of national contexts. Thus an international perspective is essential, to consider the findings of such disparate measures as work-sharing initiatives in Belgium, Sweden's national partial pension scheme, overtime reduction in the Netherlands, West Germany's experience with short-time working and the embryonic development of job-sharing in the United States. The purpose is not to discuss all aspects of working time systematically across all countries but rather to highlight the main patterns and trends and the most significant changes. Only by tackling the subject in this way can an adequate picture emerge of the range of innovations taking place and their relative importance. With the author based in Britain, some bias towards working time developments there has proved unavoidable, if only because of the fuller access to information on developments in Britain; however, in a number of aspects the more significant changes have been occurring elsewhere, and these have been given as much attention as a broad approach such as this one allows.

Many of the subsequent chapters focus on a particular aspect of working time, examining the significance of recent changes (and in some cases the lack of change) and the implications for the arguments challenging existing worktime patterns, reviewed above. The pattern of weekly hours is the subject of Chapter 2. Given its centrality to the overall structure of working time, the development of weekly hours is considered in some detail, with changes in Britain being compared to those occurring in other capitalist and non-capitalist societies. This chapter also includes a consideration of the work-sharing debate, and in particular the arguments for and against work-sharing, the shortcomings of those arguments and the results of recent work-sharing initiatives and working hours changes. Several of the issues raised in this section are also relevant to other aspects of working time discussed in subsequent chapters.

The relationship between normal weekly hours and total hours worked annually is affected mainly by the amount of overtime worked and the extent of holiday entitlement; these are the subjects of Chapters 3 and 4. In Chapter 3 the pattern of overtime working is reviewed and the reasons for overtime working discussed. An understanding of these reasons, emanating both from management and workers, is necessary in order to judge both the often-voiced calls for reducing overtime and the criticism of work-sharing that reduced hours would lead to higher overtime rather than greater employment opportunities. Overtime is a means of extending the length of the working day. Another way of achieving this same end is by the introduction of a shiftwork system; overtime and shift-work may be seen by management as alternatives and it is appropriate to consider them together. Chapter 3 therefore also examines some of the main shiftwork patterns in operation, the health and social implications of shiftwork, the recent development of new patterns and the overall prospects for the growth of shiftworking. In Chapter 4, a brief account of the historical development of holi-days is followed by a summary of recent trends including the prospects for an extension of sabbatical leave; the latter has been seen as a potentially important means of breaking existing barriers between the mixing of education and work. Short-time working is examined in Chapter 5. Given the element of work-sharing con-tained in short-time working, the development of this practice as a response to recession in Germany, Britain and North America sheds additional light on the work-sharing arguments raised earlier.

One of the most significant changes in worktime patterns in the last 20 years has been the marked growth in part-time working. The extent and reasons for this growth are discussed in Chapter 6, together with the early development of job-sharing. Other varia-tions on the standard work week are discussed in Chapter 7, in par-ticular the development of flexible working hours or 'flexitime', and the experience of compressed week working and staggered working hours. In Chapter 8, developments in retirement provision are considered, including changes occurring in retirement age and the degree of choice over aspects of the retirement decision includ-ing both the age and *rate* of retirement. In this chapter as in preced-ing ones, attention is paid to the actual degree to which individual discretion has been extended over this aspect of working time, and what has been the outcome of any such extension. The concluding chapter examines the future prospects for working time drawing together themes discussed in previous chapters, and reappraising the arguments for extending the degree of choice over individual worktime arrangements.

As has been noted, the subject of working time is broad, for in addition to its various differentiated components, it is also con-nected indirectly to several other major aspects of the organization of work. The present book concentrates on the patterns of different aspects of worktime, the recent changes occurring and some of the implications of those changes. However, given the breadth and interrelated nature of the topic it is appropriate at the outset to note those areas which regrettably have had to be left out. These include domestic work, temporary work and the pattern of worktime in non-industrial societies.

The domestic sphere requires, and deserves a much greater analysis than would be available here and the author can do no more than encourage the reader to look beyond the more traditional definitions of the workplace, and examine some of the sociological literature on domestic work roles (see for example, Oakley, 1974). The same may be said of temporary work, which since the introduction of state schemes particularly for the young unemployed, has burgeoned into a major aspect of work life in many countries. A considerable literature has developed around these schemes, much of it critical of their 'band-aid' nature in the face of continued high unemployment and lack of fully resourced youth training programmes (see, for example, Rees and Atkinson, 1982). Successfully bridging the transition from school to work is likely to remain one of Western societies' chronic problems in coming years. The scale of the problem is daunting, and the issues complex; nothing would be gained by including here what would necessarily be a sketchy account.

As the quotations at the beginning of this introduction suggest, industrialization has profound implications for notions of worktime and time discipline. Readers wishing to examine the issue of time more broadly than has been the case here would do well to begin with Hallowell's (1937) early account of time reckoning in traditional societies.

The focus on working time patterns and changes also prevents more than passing reference to the way different groups experience time at work (for example in the way Cavendish (1982) has considered women's experience of time on assembly line work). Furthermore the changes and trends considered in the following pages concentrate on the worktime patterns of waged and salaried workers rather than the self-employed. For reasons of space, such exclusions have proved necessary, though with hindsight some omissions may prove more damaging than others. But for now, enough of what has been left out; let us turn to what has been kept in, and first to the pattern of weekly hours and the debate over work-sharing.

Notes

1. The OECD, for example, has estimated that 20 million new jobs are required in its member countries in the next five years simply to hold unemployment at its present level.

2. Even when the greater overtime worked by blue-collar workers is excluded, the differences in basic hours between the two groups still represents blue-collar workers working the equivalent of two years longer than white-collar workers (see Table 2.2 in Chapter 2, below).

2 THE WORKING DAY, WORKING WEEK AND THE WORK-SHARING ARGUMENT

In analysing developments in working time it is appropriate to begin by tracing changes in the length of the working day and the working week. Before, but more particularly since the start of the Industrial Revolution, it is this aspect of working conditions which has given rise to most criticism and campaign by workers, social reformers and subsequently, trade unions. Changes in daily or weekly hours have a pronounced effect on annual (and lifetime) totals of time worked: among a workforce engaged for 40 hours per week and receiving 4 weeks annual holiday, for example, a 10 per cent cut in weekly hours yields *twelve times* the reduction in annual hours, compared to a corresponding 10 per cent increase in holiday entitlement. It is this potential for overall reduction in working time that has brought weekly hours to the forefront of the recent work-sharing debate. Hence, it is in this chapter that we must begin to examine the relative merits of the work-sharing argument for reducing and reorganizing working time to provide the basis for additional employment. This argument will be introduced here, though we return to it at several different points in the book, in connection with various changes in working time.

Before examining the pros and cons of work-sharing, however, it is necessary first to examine the pattern of daily and weekly hours, outlining the historical development, together with more recent changes.

Trends in Daily and Weekly Work Hours in Britain

Pre-Industrial Revolution

A common assumption about working time is that it has become gradually but progressively shorter throughout history, or at least from the medieval period onwards. Historical accounts of the long hours of both adults and young people are contrasted with the shorter hours prevailing today, and a linear path assumed between them. Indeed, such comparisons are used not only to demonstrate the improvement in working conditions which have taken place,

15

but also to support more sweeping arguments, including the 'redundancy' of trade unions in the humane world of the late twentieth-century work organization.

Yet in reality the pattern of hours reveals a more complex picture, containing periods when hours become longer, others when hours declined, and the two interspersed with long periods of stability in working time. Precision in mapping the early trends is hampered by a number of problems, however. There is little information, for example, on the variability of working time between workers and the self-employed and between those in agriculture compared to those in manufacture. In the early period it is this latter sector on which most information is available, though prior to the Industrial Revolution, this group represented a minority within the labour force as a whole. Further, working time in manufacturing is likely to have displayed a considerably different pattern to that in agriculture, where changes in the amount of daylight, the pattern of cultivation and the weather all affected (and still affect) the length of the working day. Even in manufacturing the day seems to have been variable, particularly where small-scale, domestic and outwork industries existed (Thompson, 1967). Hours of work on some days (notably Mondays) tended to be less than on days later in the week. 'The work pattern was one of alternative bouts of intense labour and of idleness, wherever men were in control of their own working lives' (Thompson, 1967, p. 73).

The problem of summarizing the early trends is further complicated by differences of opinion among economic historians. In his *Six Centuries of Work and Wages*, for example, J. E. Thorold Rogers asserts that, for the medieval artisan in Britain, 'the hours of work were not long. They seem to have been not more than eight hours a day . . .' (Rogers, 1906, p. 180). As discussed below, for Rogers, the late nineteenth century demand in Britain for an eight hour day was thus merely a call for the restoration of an earlier practice.

In what remains the most comprehensive study of working time in Britain's manufacturing industry, Bienefeld (1972) also points to fluctuations in work hours, rather than simply a progressive reduction. During the period between the fourteenth and eighteenth centuries, the fluctuations are primarily connected with changes in the number of holidays and half-holidays, these being extended in the earlier period and later, drastically reduced (see Chapter 4, below). In terms of daily work hours, Bienefeld identifies a broad stability over this period, though with certain exceptions. The changes that did occur are seen to be related to changes in real wage levels; during times of increasing wage levels, as in the fifteenth century, there was a tendency for hours to fall. This reduction in hours was sufficient, in fact, for the state to issue two Statutes (in 1495 and 1515) defining the working day, thereby seeking to reverse the trend towards fewer hours. Under these Statutes the working day was defined as between 5 in the morning and between 7 and 8 in the evening, with 2½ hours for meals. In documenting the 'Struggle for a Normal Working Day', Marx (1976) comments that in practice these Statutes were not strongly enforced, with the result that labourers' hours continued to be more favourable than those specified in the Statute book.[1] By the mid-sixteenth century, any pressure for reduced hours appears to have receded and for the next two centuries the pattern of weekday working hours remained little changed.

Following Bienefeld's analysis, the rise in real wages in the eighteenth century was a major factor behind the proliferation of a working day lasting from 6 a.m. to 6 p.m. (with two hours for meal breaks). This 10 hour pattern appears to have become generally accepted as the normal working day at this time. In the minority of cases where continuous shifts operated (e.g. in iron-making), 6 to 6 similarly acted as the basis of the shift system.

The Early Nineteenth Century

The main exception to the general establishment of a 10 hour working day was the textile industry, and in particular, cotton manufacture. Rather than a decrease in hours, the last quarter of the eighteenth century witnessed hours *increasing* to a general level of 12 per day (6 a.m. to 7 p.m. with one hour break); particular regions worked up to 13½ hours per day (Bienefeld, 1972, p. 32). It was these longer hours in textiles, and specifically the hours worked by women and children, which gave rise to the long-fought campaign to secure parity of a 10 hour working day. The Ten Hours reformers secured several Acts of Parliament (e.g. in 1802 and 1819), but these remained largely unenforced; it was not until an Act in 1847 that hours of women and children in textiles were brought broadly into line with average hours worked elsewhere. This legislation remains one of the landmarks of political reform in Britain on the question of working hours; subsequent changes in hours have primarily resulted from collective bargaining, following the rise of the trade union movement towards the end of the nineteenth century.

Outside the textile industry, the pattern of hours in manufacturing was characterized by stability rather than change. It is important to remember, however, that the spread of the factory system at this time, and the greater time discipline that this entailed meant for many people 'increases in the regularity and intensity of work . . . [and] . . . implied increases in annual hours for most men' (Bienefeld, 1972, p. 80; see also Thompson, 1967).

A Note on Saturday Working

The amount of hours worked each week was determined not only by daily totals but also the extent to which Saturdays were treated as exceptional. In fact, the number of hours worked on Saturdays appears to have reflected other changes occurring in daily hours — broadly, some reductions in hours on Saturday during the fifteenth century, followed by an extension of Saturday working and later, a gradual reduction. Bienefeld suggests that in the early medieval period the practice of finishing work at midday on Saturday was common both in Britain and abroad (p. 16). However, the increasing practice of paying the shorter Saturday at less than a full day's rate, together with the Puritan purge on holidays in general, reduced the Saturday half-day to a rarity by the eighteenth century. Saturday working of slightly shorter than a full day reappears in certain industries and regions in the nineteenth century, though often this represented a compression of the working week rather than shorter hours, the unworked hours on Saturday being 'made up' by longer hours during the week. The shorter Saturday became increasingly common in the latter part of the nineteenth century. and may have spread in Britain somewhat earlier than abroad. Evans (1975, pp. 86–7), for example, notes that in industrialized countries as a whole, the short Saturday tended to be introduced concurrently with, or soon after, the introduction of the 48 hour week, which had only become widespread in Europe by the 1920s (patterns of working hours outside Britain are examined, below).

The Late Nineteenth Century

In the latter half of the nineteenth century, the major changes in work hours were concentrated in the short period 1872–4, though pressure for a nine hour day had been developing since the 1850s (an abortive Nine Hours Movement had sprung up in 1858, for example, organized by the London Building Trades). The early 1870s witnessed the coincidence of an economic upswing, a growth in craft unionism, low levels of unemployment, and a series of strikes over shorter hours. Collective bargaining between employers and the craft unions over working hours became widespread, with the result that by 1875 the 54 hour week was common (comprised of either six 9 hour days or longer weekdays and a shorter Saturday); the 6 to 6 pattern remained typical in continuous shiftworking operations.

Following the changes in 1872–4, the working day appears to have remained virtually unaltered until 1919, though this was not for want of trying on the part of both employers and the growing trade unions. The onset of recession after 1875 saw an employers' offensive to lengthen the working day. Whilst increases in hours were introduced in certain industries — for example, parts of the engineering industry (see Burgess, 1975, p. 45) — overall the offensive appears to have been fairly successfully contained by the trade unions, and some of the ground lost by the unions was subsequently recovered during the upturn in trade in the early 1880s (Bienefeld, 1972, pp. 117–8). Littler (1982) also notes that the more extensive use of systematic overtime during this period moderated employer pressure to lengthen the normal day; so much so that whilst 'the nine-hour day held up *in name* during the Great Depression . . . the formal position disguises considerable forced overtime working' (p. 76; italics in original).

Union pressure for changes in hours during the 1880s and 1890s, took the form of a renewed demand for an eight hour working day. This had been advocated by Robert Owen as early as 1817, and later in 1866, the claim for an eight hour day was adopted by the International Workingmen's Association (the First International) at its congress in Geneva. In Britain, it was in the late 1880s that pressure for an eight hour day really mounted. The demand became an important rallying call for the newly-forming mass trade unions. This demand was given early credibility by the publication (in 1884) of Thorold Rogers' *Six Centuries of Work and Wages*. According to this historian and Member of Parliament, the claim for an eight hour day was a claim for *restoring* an earlier pattern of work. 'The artisan who is demanding an eight hours' day . . . is simply striving to recover what his ancestor worked by four or five centuries ago' (Rogers, 1906, p. 543).

In addition to representing a claim for a share in the fruits of industrial growth, the demand for shorter hours was also couched in terms of ensuring more regular employment and a reduction in numbers unemployed. 'The juxtaposition of long hours with high unemployment gave rise to the belief that a general limitation of the working day would automatically lead to the absorption of the unemployed' (Harris, 1972, p. 59). The Eight Hours movement in Britain in the 1880s and 1890s, however, was unsuccessful: the eight hour day was not generally introduced until well into the next century. Nevertheless, the arguments voiced, both for and against — particularly those linking shorter hours with lower unemployment — bear a close resemblance to the current work-sharing debate, and as such warrant closer examination.

The main proponent of the eight hour day (and its employment creating potential) was Tom Mann, the first Secretary of both the Amalgamated Engineering Union and the Independent Labour Party. Mann founded the Eight Hours League in 1886, though his belief in the work-sharing effects of shorter hours can be traced back much further to his apprenticeship in a Birmingham tool-making company in the early 1870s, which moved from a 10 to a 9 hour day/54 hour week, during his time there.

> The reduction of working hours to nine a day, coupled with the stoppage of overtime, had a very important bearing on my life. The firm having agreed to pay extra for overtime, very astutely gave orders immediately for a considerable extension of the factory, sufficient to accommodate an additional hundred men and boys. This was exactly what the men had aimed for (Mann, 1967, p. 5).

Leaders of the new unions of unskilled workers advocated legislation to effect an eight hour day, though the more established craft unions favoured a voluntarist approach, via collective bargaining. The TUC had noted a link between shorter hours and increased employment as early as 1869 (Hadfield and Gibbins, 1892, p. 34) and having passed several resolutions in favour of an eight hour day during the 1880s, resolved in favour of legislation on the issue in 1890 (Harris, 1972, p. 64). Mann's belief in the shorter day as a job creating mechanism was supported by Sidney Webb in a book published with Cox in 1891. 'The first effect of any reduction in hours in many industries would be an increase in the number of workers . . . some of those now working excessive hours would do less; and some now working irregularly or not at all might find an opportunity for doing more' (Webb and Cox, 1891, p. 107).

In the event, however, the Movement's work-sharing argument was severely undermined by several publications from a number of employers who, having introduced an eight hour day, concluded that total production was not affected and thus no demand to take on extra labour, created. In conjunction with Gibbins, for example, Hadfield (an early owner of the Sheffield steelworks of the same name which later became a focus of picketing activity in the 1980 steel strike) published *The Shorter Working Day* in 1892, which cited a number of examples (taken from engineering, chemicals and gas production as well as Hadfield's own steel foundry) which demonstrated that a shorter day had not created the necessity for increased employment. Other industrialists voiced similar findings (Harris, 1972, p. 68). Though this evidence did not dispel the eight hours concept *per se* — on the contrary, the employers made much of the benefits of producing the same output in a shorter period, via higher productivity — the work-sharing contentions made by Mann and others were seriously undermined, and this acted to reduce the power of the lobby for legislation on the eight hour day.

Indeed, the employers' findings led to a shift in emphasis among the eight hour advocates, away from the job creating potential of lower hours, towards the social benefits which would accrue to the existing workforce. By 1894, for example, Webb had moved his defence of an eight hour day from its power to reduce unemployment, to grounds of promoting health, efficiency, combination and self-help among workers (Harris, 1972, pp. 72–3). Mann, too, shifted his policies for reducing unemployment away from shorter hours and on to the extension of public ownership and public works (Harris, 1972, p. 71). For the Eight Hours movement as a whole, the result of the employers' experiences was a diffusion of focus, a decline in pressure (particularly for legislation) and a shift in trade union priorities on to other aspects of pay and conditions, until the question of hours once more became prominent in the years immediately following the First World War.

Twentieth-century Changes in Work Hours

Changes in weekly hours in Britain during the present century have been concentrated into four short periods: 1919–20, 1946–49, 1960–2/64–6 and 1979–82. In general these periods saw the introduction of the 48, 44, 40 and 39 hour normal working week ('normal' here and below refers to the standard working week, excluding overtime). Commenting on the first three periods, Bienefeld (1972, p. 160) notes that of the total changes in normal weekly hours between 1890 and 1965, 90 per cent occurred during these three periods. Why should hours reductions be relatively rare occurrences and be concentrated in a series of steps rather than as a steady decline? There are a number of possible explanations. It may, for example, reflect workers' and unions' predominantly higher priority towards increasing income rather than reducing time, particularly during times of price rises. Further, Bienefeld suggests that where both objectives are sought, the income objective will usually take precedence since 'the opposition of leisure preferers to an increase in income is likely to be much less strong than that of income preferers to an increase in leisure' (p. 177).

Related to this, demands for hours reductions have often tended to be sought by unions as an additional (and secondary) demand to that of a wage increase. Over time this may have acted to turn hours reductions into a 'Cinderella' item on bargaining agenda, disappearing as the focus on the primary demand sharpens. The effect of this could be a gradual tendency for hours issues to be taken less seriously by management, in the knowledge that in the past, claims for shorter hours had been dropped as agreement on wages approached.

Given these (and other) factors potentially acting against bargained reductions in hours, what has characterized the periods during which hours *have* fallen? That the first three periods were ones of rising real wages may account for unions turning their attention elsewhere than wages (Bienefeld, 1972). To this we may add the pressure of postwar expectations (re. the first and second periods), substantial rises in productivity (notably in the 1960–66 period) and the fear of unemployment (influencing reductions after 1979). More general factors facilitating reductions in normal weekly hours in the twentieth century include the increased use of shiftworking and the reliance on overtime (see Chapter 3).

Looking at the last decade in Britain in more detail, there was virtually no change in average normal hours between 1975 and the beginning of 1979. However, subsequent years witnessed a greater activity in this area, with over seven million manual workers experiencing a reduction in hours between 1980 and 1983 (Table

Table 2.1: Changes In Normal Weekly Hours of Manual Workers In Britain, 1976–1983

Year	Number of workers affected (000s)	Average reduction in hours of those affected
1976	7	1.0
1977	3	1.3
1978	127	2.5
1979	35	5.3
1980	489	1.2
1981	3,230	1.0
1982	1,949	1.1
1983	1,614	1.1

Source: Department of Employment 'Recent Changes in Hours and Holiday Entitlements', *Employment Gazette*, **92** (4), April 1984, p. 174.

2.1). By December 1983 the average normal weekly hours of male manual workers in Britain was 39.2 hours, a fall of almost three-quarters of an hour since 1979. In terms of normal hours (i.e. excluding overtime) this represents a partial 'catching up' by male manual workers over their non-manual counterparts; to a smaller extent the same is true for manual and non-manual women. However, as Table 2.2 indicates, significant gaps still exist between the hours of manual and non-manual workers, particularly when overtime working is taken into account (overtime is discussed separately in the following chapter).

Differences are also apparent within, as well as between, the categories shown in Table 2.2. For example, whilst the normal week of manual workers declined overall by 0.7 hours between 1979 and 1983, this masks considerable variation. On the one hand there are those groups (probably between a quarter and a third of the total manual workforce) who by 1983 had not achieved a reduction in weekly hours below 40 — agricultural workers, for example, and many male workers in the health service, food and drink industry, clothing and textiles (Trades Union Congress, 1983c). In contrast, a significant number of manual groups had bargained their hours substantially below 40, by 1983. Of the 73 collective agreements on shorter hours monitored by the TUC during 1983, 19 involved a reduction to 37 hours or below, and a further 10 involved a reduction to 37½ hours (TUC, 1983b and c). The degree of variability in total weekly hours (i.e. normal hours plus overtime) within male manual and non-manual groups, and the extent

Table 2.2: Normal Weekly Hours, Overtime and Total Weekly Hours in Britain, April 1975–April 1984

	Manual men			Non-manual men			Manual women			Non-manual women		
	Normal hours	Average overtime hours	Total weekly hours	Normal hours	Average overtime hours	Total weekly hours	Normal hours	Overtime hours	Total weekly hours	Normal hours	Overtime hours	Total weekly hours
1975	39.9	5.6	45.5	37.3	1.4	38.7	38.5	0.9	39.4	36.2	0.4	36.6
1976	39.9	5.4	45.3	37.2	1.3	38.5	38.5	0.8	39.3	36.2	0.3	36.5
1977	39.9	5.8	45.7	37.3	1.4	38.7	38.4	1.0	39.4	36.4	0.3	36.7
1978	39.9	6.1	46.0	37.3	1.4	38.7	38.5	1.1	39.6	36.3	0.4	36.7
1979	39.9	6.3	46.2	37.2	1.6	38.8	38.5	1.1	39.6	36.3	0.4	36.7
1980	39.7	5.7	45.4	37.1	1.6	38.7	38.5	1.1	39.6	36.3	0.4	36.7
1981	39.7	4.5	44.2	37.1	1.3	38.4	38.4	1.0	39.4	36.1	0.4	36.5
1982	39.4	4.9	44.3	37.0	1.2	38.2	38.3	1.0	39.3	36.1	0.4	36.5
1983	39.2	4.7	43.9	37.1	1.3	38.4	38.1	1.2	39.3	36.1	0.4	36.5
1984	39.2	5.1	44.3	37.1	1.4	38.5	38.1	1.3	39.4	36.1	0.4	36.5

Source: 1972–79, *Department of Employment Gazette*; 1980–84, *Employment Gazette.*

Table 2.3: Distribution of Total Hours of Full-time Male Employees in Britain. Selected Years, 1973, 1977, 1981

Total weekly hours	1973 Manual %	1973 Non-manual %	1977 Manual %	1977 Non-manual %	1981 Manual %	1981 Non-manual %
36 hours or less	1.3	20.8	1.5	23.0	2.0	23.9
36 to 40 hours	32.1	58.8	38.2	58.5	49.4	59.6
40 to 48 hours	33.5	14.8	32.5	12.9	28.0	12.2
More than 48 hours	33.2	5.6	27.8	5.6	20.6	4.3

Source: *Department of Employment Gazette*, October 1973, October 1977; *Employment Gazette*, October 1981.

to which this variability changed between 1973 and 1981, is shown in Table 2.3.

Thus the pattern of full-time hours in Britain continues to show a marked degree of variation not only between the sexes and between manual and non-manual grades, but also between different occupational groups within those broad categories. Later chapters will develop this picture further by elaborating, among other things, the pattern of development of overtime and part-time working. Before this, however, it is necessary to examine the development of weekly hours patterns outside Britain, and consider the degree of similarity to and divergencies from, the trends outlined above.

Trends in Working Hours Outside Britain

General Trends

In a report for the International Labour Organization on hours of work in industrialized countries, Evans (1975, pp. 6–7) argues that 'reduction of working hours have tended to follow similar trends in large groups of industrial countries, even if some among them were somewhat ahead or behind others'. Clearly there are a number of pitfalls in any such generalization; for example, on the topic of international comparisons of working time, the problem of comparable data is ever present.[2] Moreover, even where certain broad similarities between countries exist, at the same time the patterns of change in hours display a number of interesting and significant differences. For example, Evans notes that in the years after the First World War, the 48 hour week represented the general standard in Europe, Australia and New Zealand. Notable exceptions to this pattern, however, included the United States (where the downward shifts in hours came some years later in several industries) and Japan, where hours remained above 50 per week into the 1950s (both these countries are discussed in more detail below).

The rise in productivity and real incomes in the industrialized world in the generation following the Second World War created the demand, and the conditions for, a further reduction in hours (initially from 48 to 45 or 44 hours), though as Evans indicates in his comment above, considerable differences in the timing of this reduction are evident. A number of countries had in fact gone so far as to adopt 40 hours as the normal week even before the war. In France, for example, the principle of the 40 hour week (though with considerable scope for additional overtime) was established by legislation as early as 1936. Similarly, in New Zealand, arbitration tribunals introduced the 40 hour normal week in the 1930s, a pattern followed in Australia in the later 1940s (Evans, 1975, p. 22). Canada, too, had a number of 40 hour collective agreements by the early 1950s. However, as with the US Fair Labor Standards Act of 1938 (which established the point beyond which overtime premia became payable), these early legislations, agreements etc. appear more related to announcing a desired goal or establishing the basis for paying overtime, than accurately defining the actual length of the working week.

In Britain, normal weekly hours had dropped below 45 hours by 1948, whilst in Belgium, Denmark, the Federal Republic of Germany and Sweden this fall did not occur until around a decade later, and not until the early 1960s in the Netherlands (NBPI, 1970b, pp. 92–111). This pace of reduction appears to have gathered momentum in the later 1960s and early 1970s, with the effect that workers in these countries had generally achieved a 40 hour normal week by the early to mid-1970s. In several countries the fall in hours was achieved by a series of staged reductions. Austria, for example, moved from 45 hours in 1968 to 43 hours (1970), 42 hours (1972) and reached 40 hours in 1975. A similar pattern is evident in Belgium (1968: 45 hours; 1972: 42 hours; 1974: 41 hours hours, 1975: 40 hours) and in several other European countries, including Denmark, Italy, Luxembourg, Norway and Sweden (Evans, 1975, pp. 57–9; ETUI, 1979, p. 5).

In a number of countries these reductions were brought about by changes in legislation defining the normal working week; in others reductions were introduced as a result of collective bargaining

Table 2.4: The Normal Work Week in Western Europe as Determined by Law or by Collective Agreement (1983)

Country	By law (hours)	By agreement (hours)
Austria	40	40
Belgium	40	36–40
Cyprus	—	40–45
Denmark	—	40
Federal Republic of Germany	48	40
Finland	40	35–40
France	39	35–39
Great Britain	—	35–40
Greece	41	40
Iceland	40	37–40
Ireland	48	35–40
Italy	48	36–40
Luxembourg	40	38–40
Malta	40	40
Netherlands	48	38–40
Norway	40	40
Portugal	48	35–45
Spain	40	40–42
Sweden	40	$37\frac{1}{2}$–40
Switzerland	45	40–45

Source: European Trade Union Institute, *Collective Bargaining in Western Europe in 1983 and Prospects for 1984*, Brussels, 1984, p. 77.

agreements. The importance of legal definitions of working hours varies considerably from country to country. Only a few countries have little or no legislation on working hours (Table 2.4.). In some countries (e.g. Austria, Greece, Norway and Spain) the normal week resembles closely that defined by legislation, whilst in others (e.g. Netherlands and West Germany) subsequent collective bargaining has reduced the work week considerably below the maxima defined by legislation; in Britain hours legislation covers only women, young people and certain occupations (e.g. long-distance lorry driving). Whilst many factors influence the relative importance of legislation and collective agreement in determining working hours, the considerable cross-national differences in industrial relations structures (e.g. the extent and pattern of collective bargaining and coverage of trade unions) has a significant bearing on the relative importance of the two mechanisms (see, for example, Clegg, 1976, on the effects of different structures of collective bargaining).

Table 2.4 indicates that the move towards a 40 hour normal week has now been achieved in almost all European countries, and in many, collective agreements have breached the 40 hour level. As already noted, however, such broad comparisons tend to overlook significant variation between countries regarding the pace and scope of change and the means by which that change has been introduced (via legislation, collective agreement or a mixture of the two). Closer analysis of individual countries can be used to demonstrate ways in which trends of hours have departed from the British pattern, outlined above. Several different patterns are evident, for example, from a brief examination of work hours in the USA, Germany, Japan, and non-capitalist countries such as the USSR and Yugoslavia.

Individual Country Studies

The United States. In many respects the movement in hours in the United States has followed a different timetable to that typical of European countries. In the nineteenth century, workers in the US, like their European counterparts, experienced a significant reduction in hours, though in the former by 1880 the 10 hour rather than the 9 hour day appears to have been the norm (Table 2.5).

Table 2.5: Daily Hours of Work in the United States, 1830 and 1890

Daily hours of labour	Percentage of workforce in 1830	Percentage of workforce in 1880
8 to 9	5.4	5.1
9 to 10	13.5	8.8
10 to 11	29.7	59.6
11 to 12	5.4	9.6
12 to 13	32.5	14.6
13 to 14	13.5	2.3

Source: Tenth Census of the USA; table reproduced in C. Bradlaugh, 'The Eight Hours Movement', *New Review*, 1889, p. 135.

In the early twentieth century, hours fell further, though unlike in Europe the 1920s saw hours temporarily increasing in some US industries (Owen, 1979).[3] Subsequently, hours fell considerably during the Depression years 1929–34, to a point below that typical in Europe. The introduction in 1938 of the Fair Labour Standards Act further encouraged the move towards shorter hours by stipulating overtime provision (of 1 ½ times the regular hourly rate) for employees engaged on government contracts. In the first year of the Act the overtime rate became payable for hours worked in excess of 44 per week; this was lowered to 42 hours in the second year and 40 hours thereafter.

Overall, in the first half of the century, hours in the United States fell from 58 hours per week in 1901 to 42 hours by 1948 (Owen, 1979, p. 12). Thereafter a levelling off in the decline in hours occurred, and this continued during the 1970s. In the period 1968–79, for example, average work weeks (including overtime) of full-time workers in America fell by less than half an hour (Hedges and Taylor, 1980). This lack of movement is more surprising in the light of the relatively low level of paid holiday entitlement which is typical in America (see Chapter 4).

Owen (1979) has outlined a number of possible explanations for this trend in work hours in the United States. Rising real wages in the early twentieth century are identified as one possible factor encouraging the downward shift in hours by reducing the necessity for long work hours to gain a subsistence income. Explanations for the levelling off of hours, however, are more elusive. In part, this may reflect a decline in perceived utility of further leisure time, following the substantial reduction in preceding years. Owen, however, suggests that increased educational attainment after the Second World War may also have contributed to the maintenance of hours, with individuals preferring income to leisure in order to obtain a satisfactory income return from their education 'investment' (Owen, 1979, pp. 23–5). The improvement in working conditions and reduced physical effort attached to many jobs, may also have acted to reduce the demand for further cuts in hours (Owen, 1979, p. 26).

Japan. Hours of work in Japan have tended to remain significantly longer than many of its industrial counterparts in the West. Whilst a 48 hour normal week was established by legislation in 1948, by 1953 actual hours in Japan were reported as still being over 50 per week, though had dropped by 1960 (to under 47 according to Evans, 1975, p. 118, or to around 48 according to Kotaro, 1980, p. 67). Kotaro argues that Japanese work hours have tended to remain long partly due to the very low levels of unemployment prevailing throughout the country's period of rapid growth; cuts in hours were seen by management as creating further shortages of labour supply, in turn threatening overall levels of production. Japanese unions are seen to have also been ambivalent towards hours cuts, being concerned that lower hours could upset the conditions that had brought about full employment and increased wages (Kotaro, 1980, pp. 71–2). Following a period of sustained rising incomes in the 1960s and 70s, however, pressure to reduce hours increased, with the result that the work week gradually declined to just over 43 hours by 1970 and subsequently fell further. A survey in 1972 found 42 hours to be the standard for 44 per cent of Japanese workers. This same survey, however, found that for more than a quarter of workers in Japan (particularly those in the food and tobacco, lumber and construction industries), a 48 hour week was still the standard (Evans, 1975, pp. 31–2). In addition the average annual hours of Japanese workers have remained longer than their European counterparts in part because of the tendency for employees in Japan to work some of their annual holiday entitlement (see Chapter 4 below).

In conjunction with the gradual reduction of working time, the five day week gradually became more common in Japan. This change has been introduced in stages, with companies initially operating one five day week per month, and gradually increasing the frequency. To improve recruitment and retention of labour appear to have been major factors bringing about the spread of the two day weekend, though subsequent studies have identified some additional improvement in attendance, productivity and accident rates (Kotaro, 1980, pp. 79–81).

Federal Republic of Germany. Whilst a law has existed in Germany since 1938 defining the maximum normal week as 48 hours, subsequent collective agreements have progressively brought about reductions from this level. These reductions occurred more gradually than in Britain, however, and at different rates in different industries. Agreed hours in parts of the manufacturing sector, for example, such as the electrical engineering and motor industries, fell more rapidly than other industries, particularly compared to services such as local transport and health (Bolle *et al.*, 1981).

Average hours in different industries dropped from 48 to 45 in a single step (though implemented at different times between 1956–8); overall average hours fell further to 44 hours in 1961–2, 43 hours in 1963, 42 hours in 1965 and 41 in 1968–9 (Evans, 1975, p.26). By 1972, 78 per cent of wage earners and 54 per cent of salaried employees enjoyed a normal week of 40 hours. These proportions illustrate an unusual characteristic of working time in Germany: the tendency for many non-manual grades to have been subject to a longer normal week than their manual counterparts. This variation is long-standing. In the late 1920s, for example, whereas three-quarters of blue-collar workers in major industries worked a normal week of 48 hours or less, public officials were subject to a 54 hour normal week (Evans, 1969, p. 40; see also NBPI, 1970b, p. 102). Recently, there has been some catching up by white-collar grades as an increasingly large proportion of the total workforce became clustered around the 40 hour level (it is also important to remember that normal weekly hours do not reflect the incidence of overtime working, typically undertaken dispropor-tionately by blue-collar grades).

Whereas shorter weekly hours, and in particular the 40 hour week, was the main focus for working time negotiations by German trade unions in the 1960s, attention shifted in the 1970s to seeking longer paid holidays. The issue of hours, however, and in particu-lar the demand for a 35 hour week, again rose to prominence in West Germany in the early 1980s. A dramatic manifestation of this demand came in the engineering industry in 1984 where members of the union, IG Metall, struck in support of 35 hours, virtually halting the vehicle producing industry. An arbitrated settlement was eventually reached involving an average cut in weekly hours to 38½ from 1985; a similar agreement was subequently adopted in the printing industry, where members of the printing workers union (IG Druck) had also taken strike action over shorter hours. Together, these settlements represented a major breach in the 40 hour standard hitherto prevailing in West German industry.

The USSR, Yugoslavia and other Non-capitalist Countries. The development of working hours in the USSR diverges in a number of ways from the patterns found in the West, most notably in the former's early adoption of a working week below 45 hours. Prior to the Revolution, working hours appear to have been compara-tively long in the USSR. Legislation in 1897 had reduced the working day in industry to 11½ hours and by 1913 the average day was still almost ten hours for six days per week (Solovyov, 1962, p. 32). In 1917, an eight hour day was decreed by the new government, and this was followed a decade later by the gradual

Table 2.6: Normal Weekly Hours of Work in Eastern Europe (early 1980s)

Country	Normal hours
Bulgaria	42½
Czechoslovakia	46 (in practice 42½ max)
German Democratic Republic	43¾
Hungary	42
Poland	46 (in practice 42)
Romania	46
USSR	41
Yugoslavia	42

Source: International Labour Office, *Working Time: Reduction of hours of work, weekly rest and holidays with pay*, ILO, Geneva, 1984, Table 1, pp. 55–60.

introduction (between 1927 and 1933) of a 41 hour week, comprising five 7 hour days, plus 6 hours on Saturday.

Weekly hours of work were temporarily lengthened (to 48 hours) during the Second World War and the period of reconstruction; however, between 1956 and 1960 the 7 hour day, 41 hour week was reintroduced. According to Solovyov, all wage and salary earners in the USSR were working the legal standard of 41 hours by 1960, with certain branches of activity (e.g. underground workers) working fewer hours. In recent years, the main change in working time in the USSR has been some compression of the working week by the development, from around 1967 onwards, of a five day week, introduced in conjunction with proportionate lengthening of weekday hours. The five day week was also progressively introduced in several Eastern European countries during the 1960s, including Bulgaria, Czechoslovakia and the German Democratic Republic. Total weekly hours in Eastern European states, however, have tended to remain marginally longer than those prevailing in the USSR (Table 2.6).

One country where the effects of weekly hours reductions were carefully monitored is Yugoslavia where a reduction from 48 to 42 hours for both blue- and white-collar workers took place between 1965 and 1971. This followed a two-year experimental period in over 400 undertakings, to measure the effects on output (Vekic, 1970). According to Lydall (1984), weekly hours in Yugoslavia are usually worked in five eight hour shifts, beginning at 6 or 7 a.m., with a four hour shift on Saturday; a statutory half-hour break means that actual hours are no more than 7½ per day. This early start to the working day is long-standing and has been criticized for its contribution towards lateness and absenteeism. The early start remains popular among workers, however, partly because it facilitates dual job holding, particularly among many small farmers who combine agriculture with factory work (Lydall, 1984, p. 243). The transition to a five day week appears to have been far from smooth in Yugoslavia. The President of the Yugoslav Federal Commission for Working Hours, for example, commented that the introduction of a five day week 'has led, in certain cases, to confusion, losses and even indignation among those who have suffered as a result . . . This has occurred most frequently in the case of certain public and other services' (Vekic, 1970, p. 260; see also the discussion of compressed workweeks in Chapter 7 below).

Current and Future Trends in Weekly Hours

In very recent years the pace of reduction in weekly hours in Europe appears to have slowed somewhat, at least temporarily, though variations between companies, industries and countries make generalizations difficult. Some reductions have continued to occur, however. At the national level, for example, certain countries who maintained longer than average normal hours during the 1970s (e.g. Greece, Switzerland and Spain) moved progressively towards a 40 hour normal week in the early 1980s. France, too, reduced the normal week from 40 to 39 hours in 1982; taken in conjunction with collective agreements, this meant that normal hours of work for manual workers in France declined by 1½ hours between 1981 and 1983 (and by just over 1¼ hours for non-manual workers) (ETUI, 1984, pp. 85–6).

Other reductions have been confined to particular sectors, industries or occupational groups. In Germany the 38½ hour agreement for engineering and printing workers has already been noted; in Belgium recent hours reductions in the private sector have brought many workers into line with their public sector counterparts on 38 hours (ETUI, 1984, pp. 81–2). Examples of other agreements reached include a 38 hour week for Dutch rail and French metal and chemical workers, and marginal changes in manual and/or non-manual hours in different industries in Italy (banking), Ireland (printing), Sweden (workers on discontinuous shifts) and Switzerland (engineering) (Incomes Data Services, 1984b; ETUI, 1984).

From the standpoint of 1985, it is evident that a number of trade unions and their federations in Europe, North America and Australia continue to put the demand for a shorter working week relatively high on their negotiating agenda. In most cases the claim is for a 35 hour week, with certain union confederations (for instance the Norwegian LO) also pursuing a harmonization of working time between manual and non-manual workers. The 35 hour week is acting as a target in the same way as the 40 hour week did in the 1960s. A number of unions, however, have already voiced their desires for an even shorter week. The Dutch union federation (FNV), for example, has resolved to 'aim towards a 32 hour week by 1990' (Incomes Data Services, 1984b). The Canadian Labour Congress has similarly voiced its support for a 32 hour standard week (Meltz *et al.*, 1981, p. 71).

If the generally low level of inflation prevailing in the early 1980s continues, pressure on trade unions to give sole priority to wage rises is likely to be reduced. Further, if real income among those in employment increases (as has been the case, for example, among many medium and high earnings groups in Britain), this could further stimulate demand for a reduction in work hours and an increase in leisure time. Moreover, having won significant increases in holiday entitlement in recent years, the focus of many work groups (though perhaps excluding the United States, where paid holidays have remained low) is likely once again to return to weekly hours. The engineering strike in West Germany in 1984 demonstrated the high degree of solidarity among the workforce towards the shorter hours issue (in two regions where figures were published around four-fifths voted in favour of the strike). With labour productivity generally increasing at an above average rate and with new technology applications offering further substantial increases in productivity, the stage appears set for union attempts to seek part of the rewards from increased productivity in the form of cuts in weekly hours.

The main factors potentially acting against such a development would seem to be first, the earlier cuts in working time (increased holidays etc.), which could lower the perceived desirability of further reductions; and second, the decline in relative power of trade unions who, as a result of falling memberships (due to unemployment) may lack the strength to press home demands for a shorter working week. On balance, however, the pursuit of a shorter working week looks likely to regain momentum. For in addition to the above factors acting to stimulate demands for reduced hours, there has also developed apparent widespread support in trade union circles for the argument that reduced working time could act to reduce, or at least offset the increase in, unemployment. With unemployment appearing set to remain high at least into the 1990s, these calls for work-sharing are likely to become increasingly strong, giving further support to demands for cuts in hours. But how strong is the work-sharing argument, and what have been the results of initiatives taken so far? These and related questions are central to much of the current debate on working time.

The Work-sharing Debate

We described above how, in the late nineteenth century, the case for an eight hour day was couched, at least initially, in work-sharing terms; i.e. that the reduction in hours would have a job creating (and job maintaining) effect. Examples of the work-sharing argument can be traced back even further. More than half a century earlier (1824), for example, the Provident Unions of Shipwrights of the Port of London resolved

> that every member of the union will not engross a greater share of work than what he can accomplish by working regular hours, vis: not before six o'clock in the morning, nor later than six in the summer evening; and that no candle work be performed after the people on the outside have left work, so that every opportunity may be given to those out of employ (cited in Webb and Webb, 1902, p. 341).

Similar arguments were made during the Ten Hours Movement, and later, during the Depression in the 1930s. In recent years, the growing and seemingly intractable problem of unemployment has again brought forth calls for work-sharing[4] measures. At these different points in history, the common claim by advocates of work-sharing has been that the reduction of hours of those in employment would create a shortfall in labour supply; as a result, enployers, in order to maintain levels of output, would be required to take on additional labour. Hence, spreading the available work is seen as a response to a situation in which the total volume of work being offered is insufficient, or at least that the volume of work is growing at an inadequate rate to maintain full employment.

In the past decade the serious problem of unemployment has given rise to calls for a variety of responses, of which work-sharing has been one. Recent advocates of work-sharing (and others) have argued the importance of recognizing the multi-causal nature of the current unemployment problem. As well as recession and deflationary economic responses, the long term transformation of former labour-intensive industries is seen to have contributed to unemployment, together with the continued expansion of working population in many societies, and the growth in competition from newly industrializing countries. Added to these is the factor of technological innovation and in particular the potential labour-saving capacity (in both office and shopfloor) of microelectronic and computer technologies. In sum, these factors are seen to have created conditions under which the problem of unemployment is no longer solvable by traditional economic strategies, without also introducing major modifications to existing worktime patterns (Hughes, 1978a; Jenkins and Sherman, 1979; Blyton and Hill, 1981; Blyton, 1982b; Leontief, 1982; Handy, 1984; Jones, 1985). Thus the main basis of the work-sharing argument is that the current problem of unemployment is not solely explicable in terms of the post-1973 oil crisis or post-1979 economic recession, but is also influenced by a serious of long term changes which are affecting the future pattern of demand for labour. The result of these is seen to be that, under present working arrangements, the projected growth in demand for labour will fall far short of the total number of people looking for paid employment.

Economists' Views of Work-sharing

In recent years the work-sharing argument has received growing attention from economists and generated increased discussion, comment and criticism in trade union, employer and government circles. The dictum which states that if two economists are brought together the outcome will be at least three opinions, holds true in the area of work-sharing. Considerable disagreement exists on the theoretical job creating potential of a reduction in hours, as well as the various factors which may mediate that relationship. Various economists (e.g. Brittan, 1983) have challenged the basic premise of work-sharing, arguing that it is based on an erroneous 'lump of labour' concept, i.e. that there is only a certain amount of labour required by an economy, and that if this is insufficient to provide work for all, the work should be spread more thinly. This is argued to be incorrect in that it understates the potential for employment growth via economic activity, and generally provides a too static view of the demand for labour. Other economists, however (for example Hill, 1983), have demonstrated that the work-sharing argument does not rely on the lump of labour concept (which is indeed too crude a portrait of the labour market), but rather is based on the premise that the current and future rate of economic growth and employment generation will (for reasons outlined above) be insufficient to create enough jobs to reduce unemployment significantly, under present working time arrangements.

On a more empirical level of analysis, macro-economists in several countries have been involved in modelling the effects of reduced hours on total employment, by utilizing computer simulations. Most of these have concentrated on the possible employment effects in national economies as a whole, of a reduction in the working week (rather than other changes in working time). Ginneken (1984) has compared seven of these models developed in the UK, Netherlands, Belgium, France and the Federal Republic of Germany. Considerable disparity is evident in their findings. Firstly, the models differ markedly in their estimates of the total employment effect of a reduction in hours. The West German model, for example, estimates a 1 per cent reduction in working time would lead to an increase in employment of between 0.6 and 0.8 per cent. Other estimates (e.g. the UK Treasury model) predict much smaller increases in employment resulting from reduced worktime (Ginneken, 1984, pp. 37–9; see also Allen, 1980). Further, particular models (e.g. the West German model and one of the two French models) conclude that other factors, such as whether or not wage levels are maintained, would have only a minimal effect on the overall degree of employment creation; others, in contrast (including the UK model and one of the two Dutch models), view the extent of wage compensation as having a marked effect on any employment increase (Ginneken, 1984, pp. 38–40). A simulation in Britain by the Department of Employment had earlier also indicated the possible mediating effects of different assumptions about productivity, overtime and output changes, following a reduction in hours (Department of Employment, 1978b).

Trade Union Responses to Work-sharing

Despite the diverse views of economists, union movements in many countries and at a number of levels have resolved in favour of work-sharing, or more precisely, in favour of working time reductions. The European Trade Union Confederation in 1979, for example, resolved to pursue a 10 per cent reduction in working time without loss of pay, via one or more of a series of possible changes:

— reducing the working week to 35 hours
— extending annual holidays to 6 weeks
— giving workers the right to a full pension at 60 years
— raising the school leaving age to 16 years and extending the right to time off for vocational training and further education (ETUI, 1979)

This resolution has been reflected in the policies of a number of national union federations and individual trade unions. The work-sharing concept may be seen to have given a wider justification to trade union claims for shorter working time; even so, negotiations have focused almost exclusively on the hours reduction side of the work-sharing 'equation', with apparently scant attention being paid to pursuing agreements about any subsequent employment creation. In Britain, the TUC inititially resolved in favour of a 35 hour week in 1972, and since the late 1970s has been monitoring and publicizing agreements over shorter hours as part of its Campaign for Reduced Working Time. Other national union federations, for example in Belgium, France, Netherlands and West Germany, have similarly paid considerable attention to working time in recent years, reflected in part in the reductions in hours which have occurred, the disputes arising over hours and the small number of (albeit limited) initiatives in work-sharing, which have been instigated (discussed below).

At the same time, the trade union movement as a whole is far from unanimous on the idea of work-sharing. There is criticism, for example, that work-sharing puts at risk the levels of income, job security, etc., of existing workforces. More specifically, unions in North America have shown considerable ambivalence, if not hostility, to temporary work-sharing measures, on grounds that these undermine long established seniority principles relating to lay-offs (see Chapter 5 below). At a more general level, trade unions continue to show little success in representing the interests of the unemployed (the major beneficiaries of successful work-sharing). The current structure of industrial relations is geared to representing the interests of capital and the *employed* workforce. Representation of the unemployed by trade unions would mark a radical departure from existing practice. Currently this lack of representation is exacerbated by the general failure among unemployed groups themselves, to organize into a coherent interest group (a variety of factors are involved here; see Schlozman and Verba, 1979; see also Blyton, 1985).

Employers' Criticisms of Work-sharing

Employers have consistently opposed the work-sharing idea in most (though not all) of its aspects. In part, this attitude is linked to trade union aims of seeking a reduction in hours whilst maintaining earnings levels. Employers and their representative organizations have argued that this would increase labour costs and thereby damage competitiveness; so much so, that the result of the reduced hours would be not an increase in employment opportunities, but a potential *decrease*, as weaker competitive positions feed through to reduced orders and lower output. This argument assumes that reduced hours would not be introduced at the same time in competing firms. If however, similar changes were made elsewhere, this would maintain relative competitive positions.

Whilst the question of costs has been the principal criticism of work-sharing among employers, other criticisms have been voiced including:

— the impracticality of blocking up unworked hours into new jobs
— the difficulty of recruiting extra skilled employees to work the hours relinquished by the existing skilled workforce
— the reduction in manpower flexibility if overtime is restricted
— the potential increase in dual job-holding if hours are reduced
— the tendency for labour supply to increase as hours fall (CBI, 1980)

Yet, whilst employers' reactions to the work-sharing concept have been predominantly negative, they have not been totally so. For example, employers in several countries (notably Germany and Britain) have at different times made extensive use of temporary work-sharing measures, involving a period of short-time working rather than lay-offs, in response to a (predicted temporary) fall in demand. For employers, this form of temporary work-sharing can have the advantage of preventing the loss of skilled workers and also avoiding costs of rehiring (see Chapter 5 below). In addition, whilst employers have criticized the demand for a shorter working week, other ways of reducing worktime have attracted more muted criticism and, in some cases (e.g. reduced overtime and a lower retirement age), qualified support (CBI, 1980). Moreover, in both Britain and abroad, there has been at least a degree of employer interest in those state early retirement schemes which have required employers to replace the retiring worker with someone who is unemployed (though at the same time it is clear that employers have used early retirement more frequently as a means of *reducing* rather than replacing manpower; see Chapter 8).

Were there to be some change in the general union position of maintaining earnings where hours are reduced, at least some employers could be expected to show a rather greater willingness to discuss work-sharing. Scope for negotiation in this area could possibly be found in the size of future *increases* in earnings, rather than the present earnings level. In the Netherlands, for example, a general framework agreement has been reached between union and employer federations, to reduce working time (by 10 per cent); part of this agreement concerns the costs being offset by unions foregoing part of the future pay rises which have in the past been indexed to rises in the cost of living. The overall work-sharing potential of this framework agreement, however, is at the present time unclear. In part, the scope for similar agreements elsewhere depends on the pattern of employee preferences concerning income and leisure, and desired trade-offs between the two.

Employee Preferences on Working Time and Time-leisure Trade-offs

Whilst the general trade union position on hours reduction without loss of earnings is fairly clear, relatively little in known of employees' own attitudes towards trading some income for a drop in hours. The economic model of this posits employees working up to the point where the value of extra income is outweighed by the desire for leisure. This offers a simple picture, yet in reality, few individuals can exercise anything other than a very limited degree of choice over their work hours-leisure pattern. For most, the institutional rigidity of the work organization imposes a standard work-time, with only a proportion of workers capable of making fairly crude choices over reductions in their hours (e.g. whether to take a full-time or part-time job, to continue or cease working over-time, to retire or continue working).

What evidence is there of employee willingness to trade income for greater leisure? The most extensive study of this remains that undertaken by Best (1980) on a sample of around a thousand workers in the United States in the late 1970s. When asked the most preferable choice between (i) longer hours and proportionally higher earnings, (ii) the same hours for present income and (iii) less hours for proportionally less income, the majority favoured their present situation, compared to around a quarter who would choose to work more and earn more, and about one in nine who preferred the work less/fewer hours option. These responses matched quite closely the answers given to a similar question asked in another US survey in the 1960s (Best, 1980, pp. 128–9). In the later survey the group preferring the work less/earn less option was not markedly different from the rest of the sample, though there was a tendency for higher earners to be more represented (Best, 1980, p. 185). Among the work more/earn more preferers, younger, less edu-cated, non-white and lower income earners were somewhat more prevalent than the average. Interestingly, there were very few differences between the overall pattern of male and female choices.

From additional questions, Best identified a greater desire for trading part of any *future* increase in pay for greater leisure, than for foregoing part of *existing* earnings for more free time. For example, when asked how they would prefer to take either a small (2 per cent) or larger (10 per cent) increase (the choices being between higher pay and one of four equivalent changes in hours), at the 2 per cent level, two-thirds of respondents (especially the higher earners) chose greater free time, particularly increased holi-days. Faced with choices over how to take the larger 10 per cent increase, responses varied considerably depending on the type of free time offered. Almost two-thirds were willing to trade at least 40 per cent of the increase for additional paid vacation or sabbati-cal leave, and over half the sample were willing to make the same trade-off for earlier retirement. Smaller proportions, however, (44 and 27 per cent) were willing to make this level of trade-off for an equivalent cut in weekly or daily hours (Best, 1980, p. 133). Summing across the different choices, Best found that only about one in six would choose to forego no part of their rise for extra free time; at the other extreme almost half indicated that they would trade the total increase for more free time (p. 134). According to Best, these findings suggest that 'American workers may be willing to forego major portions of future economic growth for more free time' (p. 135).

There is other evidence which is broadly consistent with Best's findings. Harriman (1982), for example, also identified an interest in reduced worktime options among higher income groups, such as professional and managerial employees. Other studies have indicated a preference for reduced work hours in later life (see discussion of attitudes towards retirement in Chapter 8 below). The overall pattern of attitudes, however, is likely to be far from static. In the late 1970s, for example (when Best conducted his study), attitudes towards the security of future income are likely to have been more positive than in subsequent years, in which unemployment rose dramatically. Likewise, in periods characterized by high rates of inflation, attitudes towards protecting real income levels are likely to be more prominent among individuals as well as trade union organizations, compared to pursuing greater leisure.

Moreover, contrasting evidence exists on the pattern of preferences concerning income and free time. Not all groups will prefer, or feel in a position to consider, trading income for leisure. Those in lower paid jobs, for example, and those in stages of the family life cycle which involve heavy financial commitments (e.g. child-rearing periods) are least likely to feel scope for choice over income trade-offs. On the contrary, these groups might be expected to express interest in trading leisure for greater income, rather than vice versa. Evidence from a range of enquiries appears to support this. Katz and Goldberg (1982), for example, found a strong interest among Israeli workers in working *longer* hours, particularly among the 30–40 years age group. The extent of moonlighting or multiple job-holding in countries such as the USA similarly indicates a preference among some groups for income rather than time (see, for example, Brown, 1978). The apparent lack of difficulty which British managers generally experience in finding employees to work overtime, also suggests that the relative priority attributed to free time compared to increased income, is far from universal.

At most, therefore, the available evidence suggests that *some* groups are potentially interested in reduced worktime even where this involves foregoing some income, particularly if this entails a reduction in the level of some future increase. This arrangement of foregoing part of future pay increases could come to represent a broader basis of agreement between unions and management on reduced worktime and work-sharing. Financing reduced hours at least partly by reducing the level of increases in earnings has the benefit of involving income which has not already become integrated into household spending patterns (particularly if cost of living parity is maintained). Hence, rather than the work-sharing argument becoming stalemated around the question of maintenance of earnings, greater attention might fruitfully be paid to the pattern of future increases in pay and reductions in hours.

Results of Work-sharing Initiatives and other Worktime Reductions

With the cases for and against work-sharing much contested and with no clear evidence emerging from the modelling of hours reductions, the results of work-sharing intiatives taken so far, together with any evidence of employment effects from more general working time reductions, assume an added significance. Two of the main forms of work-sharing to be introduced — temporary short-time working and certain national early retirement schemes — need only brief discussion here, since they are examined in more detail in later chapters. Both practices have met with a degree of success, though in both cases it is evident that the success is contingent upon a number of factors. Compensated short-time working schemes, for example, as an alternative to redundancies have been found to be an effective form of work-sharing where the timescale is relatively short (i.e. an economic downturn lasting a matter of months, rather than years). Where recession is protracted, short-time working is more likely simply to postpone redundancies, rather than prevent them. Yet for up to a year or even longer, spreading the available work via short-time working (coupled with some form of compensation for workless days) has been shown to have considerable benefits for employers as well as employees (see Chapter 5).

The success of national early retirement schemes, promoting work-sharing by requiring employers to replace the outgoing worker with someone who is unemployed, is also influenced by a number of factors. For example, the level of allowances paid to the early retiree is a major variable affecting take-up, especially in those situations where older workers are also covered by a private occupational pension scheme. Yet, despite the relatively low levels of allowance and limited eligibility of, for example, the Job Release Scheme in Britain, it has nevertheless demonstrated at least a degree of work-sharing potential (see Chapter 8).

Demonstrating a work-sharing effect from permanent reductions in weekly hours is much more difficult, though the extent to which the experiences to date negate the work-sharing arguments, as opposed to pointing to necessary modifications to the argument (e.g. in relation to the magnitude of hours reduction required, the timing of reductions and the measurement of work-sharing effects), is not clear. Three examples — the work-sharing initiatives in Belgium, the reduction of the working week from 40 to 39 hours in France in 1982, and a similar reduction in the British engineering industry in 1981 — illustrate the pattern of results evident so far, and the questions these results raise for the work-sharing debate.

In Belgium, the high level of unemployment led, in 1982, to a government decree, which became known as the '5:3:3' formula. This required industrial sectors to introduce reductions in working time of 5 per cent, moderate pay increases by 3 per cent and increase employment by 3 per cent.[5] In its first two years of operation, the results of this decree have been far more limited than predicted, both in terms of hours reduced and jobs created. As time has passed, estimates of employment creation have been progressively scaled down; a study conducted on the period 1983/4 found that only around 29,000 jobs had been created as a result of the 5:3:3 policy — less than half that estimated by the Belgian government and only a fraction of the total unemployed (European Industrial Relations Review, 1985). This study also showed that hours had fallen less than anticipated and the extent to which savings on pay had been translated into hours cuts or additional employment, much lower than originally expected.

A fairly similar picture is evident in the French experience with introducing a 39 hour normal week (down from 40 hours) at the beginning of 1982. A study by Marchard and colleagues estimated that by September 1982 the reduction in hours had led to between 10,000 and 20,000 new jobs in industry and between 4,000 and 8,000 new jobs (mainly part-time) in commerce (study cited in Ginneken, 1984). These figures were markedly below those suggested by a French macro-economic model of the employment effects of cuts in hours (Ginneken, 1984, pp. 38–9). Among the possible reasons for the discrepancy are a greater than expected level of substitution of capital for labour following the hour reduction, an increase in work pace, slightly higher rates of overtime, and a tendency for some (mainly small) firms to respond to the reduction in hours by cutting output (pp. 48–9).

Evaluations of hours reductions in Britain have also failed to demonstrate a significant job creating potential. In their extensive study of engineering, for example (where weekly hours were reduced from 40 to 39 in 1981), and printing (hours reduced to 37½), White and Ghobadian (1984) found that increases in labour productivity had been sufficient to compensate for the effects of reduced working time. The hours reductions had coincided with, and given impetus to, a number of parallel developments in manpower utilization and technological change, the result of which was no additional demand for labour being stimulated. This confirmed earlier studies (White, 1981; 1982) and overall led the authors to the conclusion that 'the employment creating potential of shorter hours has been seriously over-estimated in the past, at least in relation to present conditions' (White and Ghobadian, 1984, p. 182).

Where do these findings leave the argument for work-sharing? Clearly any link between hours reductions and employment levels, if it exists at all, is not a simple or automatic one. The translation of hours reductions into extra employment opportunities has been shown to be low, and in many cases absent. Can a case still be made for work-sharing?

Despite the lack of supporting evidence from the studies cited above, there are a number of points which may be made in the defence of the work-sharing concept. First, many of the hours reductions which have been subject to evaluation have been small — often involving a cut of only one hour per week. Under such circumstances, a number of alternatives may be available to employers to make minor adjustments (including reducing breaks and increasing work pace) to compensate for time loss. Only in the most rigidly machine-paced of jobs is a reduction equivalent to 12 minutes per day likely to prove difficult to make up. Moreover, where reductions in hours are introduced gradually over a period of time, this extends the opportunities for employers to respond to reductions by seeking productivity increases, rather than increasing manpower levels. The importance of these factors has not gone unrecognized by trade unions. The ETUC, for example, in its demands for shorter working time, has called not only for a significant (10 per cent) reduction in working time, but also for a rapid reduction. Overall, employer responses to a small cut in hours may not be an accurate guide to the responses engendered by larger cuts.[6]

Secondly, whilst the above studies indicated the low job *creating* potential of the hours cuts studied, the reductions would also have contained a work-sharing element if there was a significant job *maintaining* effect. That is, the time reductions under consideration may have been insufficient to create jobs but may have acted to reduce the likelihood of further job loss via redundancies. This aspect of work-sharing tends to be studied much less (except in the case of temporary short-time working measures). In part this may reflect measurement difficulties, since the subject of enquiry is a hypothetical question of what would have happened if hours had *not* been reduced. White and Ghobadian (1984) suggest that there was little evidence of a job maintenance effect in their study (pp. 181–2); as the authors point out, however, the question was not studied directly.

Thirdly, the timing of the hours cuts may have acted against any work-sharing potential. There were, for example, few signs of significant recovery from recession in 1982; indeed by the time of writing (1985) recovery is evident in only some sectors, and even in those the upturn is tentative. Hence the context was not one of sustained increases in demand, but rather one of widespread uncertainty and unused capacity. Under these conditions, improvements in labour productivity are likely to be easier than where organizations are working at full capacity. A relatively large and rapid reduction in hours during a period of sustained economic growth would potentially have a much greater work-sharing effect than that demonstrated in the foregoing studies.

Fourthly, though the reductions in hours in the British engineering and printing industries were the result of collective bargaining agreements, as in the legislated reductions in France, these contained no agreement on a work-sharing response to maintaining output. Whilst it has become common for trade unions to negotiate reductions in working time, to reach 'no redundancy' agreements with employers and even to agree on temporary short time work-sharing measures, collective bargaining has not yet been generally extended to the point where agreements are made which restrict employers to increasing manpower in order to maintain production following a cut in hours, rather than introducing other changes.

Yet these arguments notwithstanding, the situation remains that the evidence so far offers little support to a direct work-sharing effect from hours reductions. In this respect the 1980s resemble the situation faced by the advocates of the Eight Hour Day in the 1890s. What these findings do is to force a reassessment of the work-sharing argument, and in particular its generalizations concerning the link between hours and employment. A more disaggregated approach is needed, to identify the relative work-sharing potential of different changes in working time among different work groups in different sectors. The personal services sector, for example (hairdressing, welfare services, restaurants, etc), is likely to show a much greater work-sharing potential than, say, assembly-line production where the possibilities for capital substitution are growing annually. Further, the work-sharing argument has focused principally on the shorter working week, yet conceivably time reductions such as early retirement and job-sharing (both discussed in later chapters) will have a much more marked work-sharing effect. Likewise, the potential for work-sharing is likely to be spread unevenly across the working population — as we have seen, some groups will tend to show more interest in trading income for time than others. A clearer picture of employee preferences over working time is required to identify those groups and those settings in which work-sharing is most likely to be successful. For, despite employers' reluctance to embrace work-sharing, and the lack of supportive evidence from recent hours reductions, 'work-sharing is not a dead issue and is likely to be a central feature of future deliberations, particularly as unemployment shows no sign of diminishing' (Jones, 1985, p. 40). We will return to the question of work-sharing at a number of points in later chapters.

Notes

1. Marx (1976, p. 382) contrasts these Statutes with the nineteenth-century Factory Acts, pointing out that the former sought to lengthen the working day, and the latter to shorten it (at least for certain groups). However, argues Marx, due to an increase in hours in the textile industry in the meantime, the later Acts were in fact seeking a similar working day to that sought by the former.

2. Some countries, for example, include short-time and part-time working in the totals (thus reducing the average hours per worker), whilst others vary on how periods of non-work, such as breaks, absenteeism and strikes are treated. Further, similarities in normal hours can mask considerable differences in actual hours worked, due to variations in overtime.

3. This picture is complicated in the US by considerable variation in hours at this time in different parts of the country. Evans (1969, p. 40), for example, notes that in 1927, normal hours were usually between 44 and 48 in the North, and between 55 and 60 in the South, where union agreements were rare.

4. The concept of work-sharing has not been applied consistently in previous discussions of the subject. In North America, for example, work-sharing tends to denote only those temporary short-time working arrangements whereby an immediate threat of unemployment is mitigated by a temporary reduction in work-time. Elsewhere, work-sharing denotes the overall concept of job creation and job maintenance via the reduction of working time by one or more of a series of measures (shorter weeks, longer holidays, reduced overtime, earlier retirement, etc). It is this latter, broader definition of work-sharing which is adopted here.

5. The required increase in employment was 2 per cent in companies employing less than 50 people. Reductions in working time were not required if companies put forward alternative plans to increase employment. Those not complying with the decree incurred a fine.

6. There are two contrasting views here, however. On the one hand, larger and rapidly introduced cuts in hours may create additional employment because of the inadequacy of employers' marginal responses (increases work pace, etc) for maintaining output. On the other hand, a large cut in hours, if this entailed a significant increase in labour costs, could provoke employers to seek further ways of substituting capital for labour, thus threatening existing levels of employment, rather than effecting their increase.

3 OVERTIME AND SHIFTWORK

This chapter deals with the two main ways of extending the length of the productive working day or week. In the latter part of the chapter the changes taking place in shiftwork patterns are considered, including the progressive extension of shiftworking and the signs of development of new shiftwork systems. This aspect of working time is not problem-free, however, hence in addition to examining the reasons for growth and its implications, some consideration is given to the potential conflict between the economic benefits of a shift system and the social and other costs incurred by shiftworkers.

Before considering the nature of shiftwork, however, attention is given to overtime working which, over a long period, has occasioned concern from both employer and union quarters. Its continued growth in several countries, and in particular its persistence during periods of economic downturn and high unemployment, has given rise to much enquiry and speculation on the various economic, organizational, technical, managerial and worker-related factors encouraging overtime. Whilst some aspects of working time have undergone various modifications in recent years, levels of overtime working, particularly in Britain, have shown a remarkable resistance to change — or more specifically, to decline.

Overtime

The maintenance of high levels of overtime in several countries has various implications, not least for the work-sharing argument discussed in the previous chapter. Overtime working can influence work-sharing developments in two ways. First, a reduction in overtime hours *already being worked* is a possible basis for some work-sharing. In Britain at the beginning of 1984, for example, more than 1.1 million manual workers in manufacturing were each working an average of 8.4 hours overtime per week — a total of almost 10 million hours overtime each week. As the case studies in the last chapter demonstrated, any simple arithmetic translation of hours cuts into jobs is an abstraction considerably removed from the realities of the workplace. The scale of overtime being worked in Britain is such, however, that if only *half* of these hours were translated into full-time jobs this would potentially create between 124,000 (of 40 hours per week jobs) and 141,000 (35 hours/week) extra positions. Second, and more important in terms of the overall impact on any work-sharing, is the 'leakage' effect which overtime could have following a general reduction in hours. The expectation that hours reduction would leak into greater amounts of overtime, has been used as a major criticism of the work-sharing thesis (CBI, 1980).

Yet the scale of current overtime working in Britain and several other countries is such that its significance extends far beyond the work-sharing debate. For almost one-third of male manual workers in British manufacturing, overtime represents a major element (both in terms of time and income) in the weekly working-time pattern. For employers, too, overtime is an expensive item of labour costs, since it is generally paid at a premium rate, varying from time-and-a-quarter and time-and-a-half, to double, treble and even quadruple-time. The costliness of this aspect of working hours means that in many organizations, the level of overtime working receives frequent attention, though with mixed (and often ineffectual) results. For our argument here, it is necessary to consider a number of related questions surrounding overtime working, including: what are the reasons for overtime working? What factors encourage overtime rather than the creation of new jobs? How does the pattern of overtime in Britain differ from that in other countries? What are the prospects for change in the near future and what are the obstacles to that change?

The Pattern of Overtime Working

Overtime may be defined as time worked in excess of 'standard' hours, which is generally rewarded either by payment at a premium rate or by subsequent time off in lieu, though a proportion of overtime goes unrewarded (and unrecorded), for example among some managerial and professional groups. Overtime is a long-established practice, as is the evidence of disputation over the working of overtime. In Britain, for example, at its founding conference in 1850, the Amalgamated Society of Engineers passed resolutions repudiating overtime. The union was particularly critical of systematic forms of overtime being worked even when trade was slack (as was the case in the late 1840s and early 1850s) which was seen to exacerbate the unemployment problem among engineering workers (Burgess, 1975, p. 18). Though the ASE failed to ban systematic overtime, the extent of overtime working appears to have declined by the 1860s (partly because the payment of higher rates for overtime had become more widely recognized), though increased again towards the end of the century. Burgess cites a Royal Commission report which indicated that in 1892, approximately five out of every six ASE members were working some overtime (p. 28). Other nineteenth-century examples of systematic (and enforced) overtime can be found in the building and cotton industries (pp. 118, 241).

In the twentieth century in Britain, overtime levels rose during wartime, though after the Second World War overtime increased progressively though undramatically over the prewar level (Whybrew, 1964). This comprised both an increase in the proportion of workers undertaking overtime and also, to a lesser extent, in the average number of overtime hours per worker engaged in overtime. In 1952, for example, just over one-fifth of all operatives in Britain were engaged in an average of 7.7 hours of overtime per week; by 1964 these levels had increased to one-third and over 8 hours per week (Bosworth and Dawkins, 1981, p. 77).

In recent years, overtime has shown quite a remarkable resilience in the face of falling output and demand in the manufacturing sector, and the rise in unemployment and spare labour capacity. In the early years of the post 1979 recession, overtime working dipped, but soon began to re-establish itself at, or near former levels (Table 3.1). Within this overall pattern, there are considerable variations between different work groups. Far more overtime is worked by men than by women, and by manual workers rather than non-manual (see Table 2.2). Overtime is also more common among 'prime age' workers, compared to their younger or older counterparts. The 'typical' high overtime worker is a male manual worker in his 30s or 40s. Variation also exists between different sectors (manufacturing, transport and communication maintaining higher overtime levels than other sectors), and in some industries at different times of the year (e.g. food processing and tourist-related concerns). Inter-industry differences in level of overtime working are also associated with differences in average hourly earnings — those industries with relatively low basic pay rates tend to maintain higher levels of overtime working (Trade Union Research Unit,

Table 3.1: Overtime Working Among Manual Workers in British Manufacturing Industry, 1976–1984

	% of all operatives	Average hours of overtime/week worked per operative working overtime
1976	32.2	8.4
1977	34.6	8.7
1978	34.8	8.6
1979	34.2	8.7
1980	29.5	8.3
1981	26.6	8.2
1982	29.8	8.3
1983	31.5	8.5
Jan. 1984	31.2	8.4

Source: *Employment Gazette,* **92** (3), March 1984.

1981). This relationship between pay rates and extent of overtime also exists at the individual level; those manual workers on relatively low basic rates tend to work more overtime than their higher paid counterparts (NBPI, 1970a, pp. 25–6). This is a relationship we will return to, later.

How does the level of overtime worked in Britain compare to that in other countries? This is not easy to determine satisfactorily. Notable sources of error include differences in the definition of a 'standard' or 'normal' week, which has obvious implications for the portion of work that is defined as 'overtime'. Furthermore, a number of countries have enacted legislation to restrict overtime (discussed further below). Whilst in some cases this action may have improved the level of data collection on overtime worked, in others it may have acted to obscure the true pattern of overtime, where local management and workers have colluded to prevent the additional time worked from being recorded.

Despite these problems, a general indication of differences in overtime is possible from various studies undertaken. For example, a survey in 1977 by the Statistical Office of the European Economic Community sought the proportion of individual workforces in the EEC who were engaged in working relatively long hours. Whilst this does not provide concrete information on overtime (due to variations in the normal working week in different EEC countries), it is at least suggestive of those countries where overtime working is relatively high or low (Table 3.2). France, Ireland and the UK stand

Table 3.2: Weekly Working Hours in the EEC Equal to or Exceeding 45 Hours

	% of workforce working 45 hours or more
Belgium	7.2
Denmark	9.4
Federal Republic of Germany	13.7
France	25.2
Ireland	20.3
Italy	15.2
Luxembourg	8.1
Netherlands	11.4
UK	18.4

Source: European Trade Union Institute, *Reduction of Working Time in Western Europe*, Part 1, Brussels, 1979, p. 49.

out as having relatively large proportions of their workforce working long hours; in contrast Belgium, Luxembourg, Denmark and the Netherlands function with lower than average levels of long hours working. In the USA, the level of overtime working also displayed a rising tendency in the postwar period, though this stabilized during the 1970s. Between 1956 and 1978, average weekly overtime hours in the US increased by just over 0.6 hours (Ehrenberg and Schumann, 1982, p. 5). Most of this rise was concentrated in the first half of the period; average overtime hours in US manufacturing in 1978 was at the same level (3.6 hours per worker) as prevailed in 1968 (Hedges and Taylor, 1980). In 1938 the Fair Labor Standards Act established the level of overtime premia at 1½ times regular hourly earnings for certain types of employee in the United States working in excess of 44 hours (reduced to 42 hours in 1939 and 40 hours in 1940). In its early years the Act covered less than 20 per cent of all employees. Its coverage has been progressively increased, and stood at 59 per cent of the labour force in 1978 (Ehrenberg and Schumann, 1982, p. 10); the main categories of workers not covered are surpervisors, salesmen, seasonal workers, state and local government workers, and various groups in service employment.

Not all countries have followed Britain in experiencing a rising level of overtime working. In the Netherlands, for example, legislation on maximum hours dating back to 1919 has been important in maintaining lower levels of overtime than in Britain (Whybrew,

1964). More recently there is evidence of a further reduction in overtime in the Netherlands (ETUI, 1979, p. 51). Yet such reductions remain exceptional and to identify why overtime levels have generally persisted or increased, it is necessary to consider the different factors encouraging overtime working.

Reasons for Overtime Working

In a recent study of engineering companies in South Wales, one of the questions the author and his colleagues put to the managing directors was why overtime working was maintained as part of the overall work pattern (Hill *et al.*, 1984). The varied responses reinforced the finding which also emerges from the literature on this aspect of working time — that overtime working fulfils a number of managerial (and worker) needs, some relating to the pattern of product demand and technological or organizational constraints, others to the nature of the workforce and the attitudes of those in the workforce towards income and leisure. Examining these factors in a little more detail indicates the degree to which these various needs can *only* be met by overtime, compared to those situations where overtime is resorted to as simply the cheapest or most convenient option.

Management Reasons for Overtime Working. From a managerial point of view we can identify at least four related groups of reasons why overtime is worked. The first may be termed 'emergencies', encapsulating many different situations including a temporary and unexpected increase in demand, a pressing order deadline, absenteeism or machine breakdown. These emergency situations are by definition both short-term and generally unforeseeable. Overtime working is seen as appropriate not only because it represents a simple and immediate response to a situation demanding additional labour input but also because it is reversible when conditions return to 'normal' (though in practice this reversibility may be somewhat problematic). The unforeseen nature of emergencies is the principal reason why even the strongest supporters of overtime reduction tend not to advocate the complete elimination of overtime — there is widespread agreement that as an instant and short-term response, overtime represents a necessary tool in the manager's manpower allocation kit.

There are, however, a variety of non-emergency reasons which can influence the decision to utilize overtime (rather than other means of extending total worktime), including a series of organizational factors. A shift system, for example, may not easily divide to match the normal weekly hours of each shiftworker (e.g. a continuous, 168 hour per week shift operation, with a four crew system, will tend to create an actual working week of 42 hours — two or three hours longer than current average normal weeks). In machine-based processes, the maintenance, cleaning and related tasks may be allocated to overtime, together with tests, repairs and other activities which could interrupt the normal flow of production if undertaken during regular hours. Given that many of these activities are regular and predictable, overtime working in these cases is fulfilling neither an emergency nor short-term function. Indeed, studies conducted on overtime show that a considerable proportion of overtime working (though precisely how large a proportion is difficult to ascertain) is regular and systematic (Whybrew, 1968; NBPI, 1970a). From his review of various data relating to patterns of work, for example, Whybrew (1968) concludes that, 'this evidence suggests that overtime is worked by the same men in the same firms in the same industries over considerable periods of time' (p. 24). The NBPI similarly reported in 1970 that the commonest reason cited by management for working overtime was to deal with normal operating requirements; in more than half (51 per cent) of companies surveyed, a main reason for overtime working was to meet the normal level of demand (NBPI, 1970a, p. 19). If overtime is being used to increase production (through greater capital utilization), or for regular maintenance, this begs the question of why premium priced work overtime is being utilized, rather than the work being brought into normal work hours schedules. For even if maintenance must be conducted outside normal operating hours a shift system for maintenance employees could be thought devisable to allow maintenance activities to be carried out. At some periods the overtime working will reflect labour shortages, particularly for certain skills. However, in times of high unemployment other reasons must be sought, notably the relative *costs* of different forms of working hours.

Though much overtime worked is paid for at a premium rate, there are several factors which can act to offset this extra cost, compared to the costs of hiring additional manpower. Increasingly prominent among these in recent years has been the growing level of 'non-wage labour costs' (NWLCs) which involve employers making payments covering, for example, holidays, pension and sickness benefit schemes, redundancies and maternity allowances. In Britain and elsewhere these costs have risen both through collective agreements (for example in the case of holiday entitlement) and as a result of legislation (in the case redundancy and maternity provision), to a point where NWLCs now account for approximately 30 per cent of the total wage bill (Hart, 1984). Given that many of these NWLCs are related to employment rather than hours, this acts to reduce the relative cost of overtime among the existing workforce, compared to hiring additional employees. This difference in relative costs is further reduced by the absence of other labour-related costs which attach to employing additional workers, such as those associated with recruitment and training. Further, in Britain, the effects of certain pay policies in the 1970s acted to prevent pay increases from being consolidated into basic pay rates, thus bringing about further (though temporary) reductions in the relative cost of overtime (which is calculated as a proportion of basic rates). Indeed, 'in the 1970s, the trends of costs and external pressures such as pay policy, were if anything consolidating the persistent use of overtime' (Trade Union Research Unit, 1981, p. 37).

Moreover, in addition to raising the NWLCs of companies, other aspects of recent legislation in Britain, particularly relating to dismissal, may also be seen to have encouraged the maintenance of high levels of overtime working. Legislation such as the Employment Protection Act may have acted not only to constrain the employer's decision to reduce manpower (by, for example, strengthening employee rights over redundancy procedures and to some extent improving the provision for employees claiming unfair dismissal), but by doing so, may have reduced employers' willingness to hire labour for what could turn out to be a short period. Overtime working is one way of circumventing the situation of hiring additional workers and then at a not much later date, being faced with overcapacity.

We have already noted the potential influence of general or specific labour shortages in encouraging overtime. However, whilst this may have been one of the reasons for the growing use of overtime in postwar Britain, the continued high level of overtime working in a situation of over 13 per cent unemployment suggests that, at a general level at least, this argument is no longer valid, if indeed it ever was; Whybrew (1968) doubts the significance of this factor even in relation to the 1950s. Some regular overtime working may indeed be due to the shortage of a particular skill in a particular location; only a small proportion of total overtime worked, however, is likely to be explained by this factor. Of much more importance is likely to be the arrangement whereby work-forces on low basic wages are given the opportunity to raise earnings by working overtime. As described above, overtime tends to be worked most by those grades and in those industries where pay rates are lower than the average. In these cases, the opportunity to increase earnings via overtime working could represent an important factor in the industry's ability to attract and retain labour, as well as preventing or dampening the level of conflict over low basic rates. This link between low pay and overtime working may also have some explanatory power at a more general level in terms of understanding why Britain operates a higher level of overtime than many other countries. In a comparative perspective, many British industries have come to be regarded as low-wage, low productivity organizations, compared, for example, to parallel industries in West Germany or the United States.

Another manpower aspect which may be encouraging overtime in the present period is management's desire to retain the results of changes introduced in recent years, in particular the widespread demanning which has taken place and the removal and reduction of many traditional job demarcation practices. Having gone through the process of demanning (and the accompanying tasks connected with redundancy and redundancy payments), the desire to prevent a return to former manning levels may act as an important influence on managers, placing additional labour low on their lists of alternative strategies for increasing output — below, for example, strategies such as purchasing additional capital capacity, changing work methods, or utilizing overtime.

Employee Reasons for Working Overtime. For management to utilize overtime rather than other options (e.g. shiftwork, or increasing manpower), this presupposes the likelihood of securing the necessary supply of workers to fulfil the overtime; this will depend on either employees having little choice over whether or not they work overtime or on a sufficient willingness among employees to trade-off leisure for greater income. On the former, there is little systematic evidence on workers' freedom to work overtime, though it is certainly true that the terms of employment of a proportion of workers stipulate overtime must be worked 'as and when required'.

Cuvillier (1984) cites a large-scale study in America which found that fewer than one in six workers could refuse to work overtime without creating difficulties for themselves (e.g. having to find a substitute), though another study in the US cited by the same author indicated that some improvement in this position may be occurring (p. 60).

On workers' willingness to trade leisure for greater income, historical and contemporary evidence suggests this desire is often present in adequate quantity for high levels of overtime to be established and maintained (and indeed, jealously guarded). Reviewing studies on willingness to work overtime, Whybrew (1968) concludes that not only are large numbers prepared to trade leisure for extra income, but also that once the trade-off has been undertaken for a period, expectations and spending patterns rise, and the reliance on overtime earnings grows, thereby increasing the level of interest in its continuation.

> There is evidence that there are usually a significant number of people who want the money that overtime represents and that the satisfaction of their desires usually creates new ones for themselves and others. Thus overtime has a self sustaining growth process which results in pressure on junior management to maintain and extend it (Whybrew, 1968, p. 52).

Who are the people who show most interest in working overtime? Firstly, most overtime is worked by men. This may reflect a variety of factors — the greater proportion of men on shift-work for example and the continuing tendency for women to carry primary responsibility for domestic activities, thus reducing their availability to work longer hours even if they wanted to. Second, it is among those age groups which tend to have the greatest financial commitments where highest levels of overtime are found (men in their late 20s to late 40s). This greater desire among prime-age workers to work more hours for higher income is not a phenomenon confined to Britain. As mentioned in the previous chapter, for example, a study of Israeli workers found the level of interest in working extra hours particularly high among prime age groups (Katz and Goldberg, 1982). In Britain, the desire among some groups of employees to work overtime has been supported by a trade union movement which, whilst voicing its support at national level for reducing overtime, at local level has shown considerable compliance with members wishing to earn higher wages by longer hours. In one study of more than 2,000 establishments, the NBPI (1970a) noted that in the majority of establishments (54 per cent) management found the unions accepted or even encouraged overtime. In a large proportion of the remainder, the unions played no part in overtime arrangements; in less than half per cent of establishments unions opposed the practice of overtime working. There is little evidence of any substantial change in this pattern in recent years. Indeed, among both management and trade union organizations, a considerable gap continues to be visible between the overtime policies as espoused by national representatives and practices operating at workplace level.

The Role of Legislation Outside Britain

Overtime levels vary considerably from one country to another and despite problems of comparability, it is evident that Britain comes high up the overtime 'league'. Unlike Britain, most other European countries have sought to restrict overtime by enacting legislation to limit the amount of overtime worked. Various types of restrictions apply, relating to daily, weekly, monthly or annual limits, or a combination of one or more of these. Examples of the different types include Luxembourg where there is a legal limit of two hours per day on overtime, Belgium where overtime is restricted to 2 hours per day, 10 hours per week, and 130 hours per year and Sweden, where restrictions of 50 hours overtime per month and 200 hours per year operate (ILO, 1984). The International Labour Office lists a total of 45 countries in which overtime is limited by legislation (ILO 1984 p. 38). In a number of these cases, the legislation is supplemented by collective agreement.

Whilst the limits imposed by legislation appear relatively unequivocal, most legislation contains extra provisions to meet 'exceptional circumstances'. It is evident that in practice the criteria for 'exceptional' (and thus the overall impact of the legislation) differs considerably from one country to another, as well as over time. Nevertheless, *de jure* restrictions on overtime appear to have been one factor creating overtime levels in many countries substantially below those existing in Britain. It may be that the existence of statutory controls obliges employers and workers to be more conscientious in establishing norms which secure satisfactory output and earnings without resorting to overtime. Similarly, the absence of legislation contributes to lowering the incentive for employers to embark on a negotiation process to introduce the changes needed to maintain production without considerable amounts of overtime (NBPI, 1970a, p. 55).

Conclusion

The picture of overtime working is one of diversity between different groups of workers, different industries and different countries. The subject has attracted a good deal of comment, particularly in Britain where overtime levels have persisted at a high level for more than two decades, thereby undermining the logic that overtime is a short-term amendment to working time patterns to meet exceptional circumstances. The reality in many cases is far removed from this, with a large proportion of overtime being worked on a regular and systematic basis. As we have seen, this high level of overtime, whilst frequently criticized by both employer and union organizations, may in fact be symptomatic of a variety of other factors in the workplace including the rising level of non-wage labour costs, the inappropriate matching of production and maintenance schedules, low basic wage rates, and the significance of raising and thereafter satisfying worker expectations (which also relates to the broader issue of the value placed by employees on more income rather than more time away from the workplace). The current situation in Britain is one where the economic costs of additional employment generally encourage the continued use of overtime rather than extra recruitment, a situation which tends to find favour both with management (many of whom are reluctant to see any major growth in manpower levels following major redundancy programmes in the early 1980s) and with many groups of workers, prepared to trade non-work hours for additional income.

This situation will tend to change eventually, for example as the overall proportion of white-collar workers (who currently work considerably less overtime) in the labour force continues to grow and as the degree of automated manufacturing processes increases. The already relatively low levels of overtime among female workers may also decline further as part-time work continues to expand, representing a cheaper way of expanding the length of the productive day. In terms of the bulk of (male) overtime in the short and medium term, however, unless legislation is introduced, collective agreements on maximum hours tightened up (both of which are unlikely) or the balance of costs between overtime and additional manpower substantially altered, then levels of overtime working in Britain are likely to remain high.[1] This will have a number of implications for both managers and workers including for the former, a reduced capability to respond to emergencies, and for the latter a continued element of insecurity and fluctuation relating to earnings levels. However, a long term solution to persistent high overtime working must tackle deep-seated aspects of industrial organization, including the tendency for countries such as Britain to have developed as a relatively low wage, low productivity country rather than a high wage, high productivity one.

For trade unions and others engaged in planning for an increase in employment as a result of reductions in the standard working week, it is crucial that these stimulants to overtime are recognized and countered. In those countries where overtime is regulated by law, the mechanism to prevent the leaking of reduced hours into greater amounts of overtime is already present, though its effectiveness appears to vary considerably. Where no legislation exists, however, such as in Britain (other than concerning women, juveniles and certain occupational categories), the prevention of higher levels of overtime working will be left to formal and informal agreements and movements in the relative cost of different kinds of man-hours. Overtime levels are not immutable, but if the present trend of rising NWLCs continues, the statements by national union and employer organizations supporting reductions in overtime working will continue to bear little resemblance to what is actually happening in the industrial workplace.

Finally, in terms of our recurring theme relating to the degree of discretion and flexibility in working time, a key question regarding overtime would seem to be the extent to which employees can freely choose to work the overtime, as distinct from it being a contractual requirement, or simply procedurally difficult to refuse. Whilst a certain amount of study on this question has been conducted in the United States, in general little is known about this aspect of overtime. This would certainly seem to be a further avenue worth exploring by those concerned to understand the persistence of high levels of overtime working.

Shiftwork

A simple definition of shiftwork is 'a situation in which one worker replaces another on the same job within a 24-hour period' (Ingram and Sloane, 1984, p. 168). Though not all-encompassing, this definition emphasizes the point that, like overtime, shiftwork is a means of extending the productive day within work organizations. And as we shall see (though the recent trend is less consistent), like overtime the extent of shiftworking has increased considerably since 1950. What are the reasons for this growth? What are the economic, social and medical implications? If shiftwork is to remain at a relatively high level, how can its negative connotations be minimized? What developments in types of shiftwork systems are occurring? What is the link (if any) between increased shiftwork and employment creation? In the space of a few pages we can aim only to address some of the questions surrounding this important aspect of working time — important not only because of its extent and growth, but also because of the conflict which appears to exist between the economic benefits of shiftworking and the social and health costs which are associated with certain shiftwork arrangements.

The Extent and Growth of Shiftworking

Writers and analysts in several countries have identified a general growth in shiftwork during the past three decades. According to the International Labour Office, 'the known figures show a constant progression in shiftwork in industrialised countries in both absolute and relative terms' (ILO, 1978, p. 19). This same study estimates the overall number of workers engaged in shiftwork to have approximately doubled between 1950 and 1974 (p. 20). In Britain, the available evidence suggests a considerable rise in shiftworking during the 1950s and 60s, followed by a much more gradual rise after 1968. In one of many publications on shiftworking, Bosworth and Dawkins (1980) maintain that the proportion of manual workers involved in shiftwork rose from one in eight workers in 1954 to one in three by 1978. New Earnings Survey data suggests a more modest rise,[2] particularly after 1968, with a temporary decline occurring in shiftwork totals between 1979 and 1982, before a recovery of the earlier trend in 1983 (Bourner and Frost, 1985).

Though a postwar increase in shiftworking has been identified as widespread, nevertheless international levels of shiftwork continue to demonstrate considerable variation. Table 3.3 indicates, for example, that among EEC members, the level of shiftwork in some countries is three or four times that in others (though because of

Table 3.3: Extent of Shiftworking in the EEC (service sector not included)

Country	% involved in shift work	Sectors with most shiftwork
Belgium	26.6	Cars, Energy, Minerals
Denmark	14	Paper, Chemicals
Fed. Republic of Germany	20	Energy, Chemicals, Metals
France	31.3	Metals, Paper, Textiles
Ireland	18.8	Textiles, Chemicals, Paper
Italy	22	Metals, Paper, Non-metallic Minerals
Luxembourg	41.5	Metals, Chemicals, Fibres
Netherlands	10.6	Food and Allied Products, Textiles, Metals
UK	30	Cars, Metals, Chemicals

Source: European Trade Union Institute, *Reductions of Working Hours in Western Europe: Part One*, Brussels 1979, p. 59.

differences in definition and measures, these figures should only be used as the basis of an approximate rather than exact comparison). In the United States, estimates of the number of people engaged in shiftwork vary between one in four workers (Lehmann, 1980) and one in six (Finn, 1981); part of the discrepancy again is due to different methods of data collection, and in particular how those workers on their day shift during the time of the study, were treated. In Japan, the overall level of shiftworking is reported to be relatively low (12 per cent of workers in the mid-70s according to the ILO), though among manufacturing workers a much higher figure (37 per cent) has been noted (Fudge, 1980).

Shiftworking continues to be concentrated in certain industries and occupations — principally among male manual workers in parts of the manufacturing sector. Industries where the incidence of shiftworking is particularly high include mining, steel production, textiles, paper, chemicals and oil-refining. In terms of occupational distribution, in Britain, New Earning Survey estimates suggest that the proportion of manual workers receiving shift premia is around two and a half times that of non-manual counterparts. The available evidence suggests, however, that the general growth in shiftwork has been accompanied by a broadening of shiftwork arrangements to increasingly involve non-manual and female workers, both in the manufacturing and non-manufacturing sectors. Amoung non-manual workers in Britain, for example, the proportion receiving shift premia increased from 5.3 per cent to 9.3 per cent between 1974 and 1983 (NES, cited in Bourner and Frost, 1985). Similarly in non-manufacturing, NES figures indicate a 50 per cent increase in the numbers involved in shiftworking between 1974 and 1983, compared to a corresponding 9 per cent increase in the manufacturing sector (ibid.).

The position of women working shifts is somewhat different since, together with young people, women have been subject to legislation which limits the amount of shiftwork they can participate in. Nightwork for women in Britain was first prohibited by Act of Parliament in 1844, and subsequently by various later Acts, most recently the 1961 Factories Act, which restricts the employment of women on shifts between 10 p.m. and 6 a.m., unless exemption from the Act has been authorized by the Secretary of State for Employment. The increase in these exemptions is one indication of the rise in shiftworking among women; between 1960 and 1977, the exemption orders increased by over 17 times, and stood at over 56,000 on the last day of 1977 (Bosworth and Dawkins, 1980, p. 39). Overall, in recent years, shiftworking among employed women in Britain has increased from 7.1 per cent in 1974 to 12.3 per cent in 1983 (NES, cited in Bourner and Frost, 1985).

Shiftwork Patterns

A number of shift systems exist and whilst some shiftworkers undertake the same shift over a long period, others rotate shifts, often changing either from one week to another, or more frequently (e.g. every two or three shifts, as under the 'continental' shift pattern). The National Board for Prices and Incomes (1970a) lists the basic shift patterns as:

Continuous 3 shifts — the entire 24 hour day, 7 day week period, generally covered by four shift crews with three crews covering any 24 hour period, with typical shift times being   6 a.m.–2 p.m.,   2 p.m.– 10 p.m., 10 p.m.–6 a.m.

Discontinuous 3 shift[3] — for example 3 crews covering the entire period between Monday and Friday.

Double Day	— e.g. a morning shift of 6 a.m.–2 p.m. and an afternoon shift of 2 p.m.–10 p.m.
Days and Nights	— one day shift and one night shift, possibly of twelve hours each.
Twilight shift	— part-time workers, particularly females, working a short shift in the evening (e.g. 6 p.m.–10 p.m.)

Within individual work organizations the shift pattern may often exhibit far greater complexity than suggested by the NBPI categories; not only may various systems operate simultaneously, but also a number may be specifically adapted to meet the constraints of particular operations. Overall, however, between the mid-1960s and the late 70s, the popularity of the different shifts altered considerably, at least in Britain. In 1964, 41 per cent of manual shift workers were engaged on a three shift system (either continuous or discontinuous), compared to 17 per cent on double days, 23 per cent on alternating days and nights and 12 per cent on permanent nights (NBPI, 1970a, p. 58). By 1978, the double day shift had become the most popular (34 per cent of shift workers), followed by three shift systems (30 per cent), alternating days and nights (24 per cent) and permanent nights (7 per cent) (Bosworth and Dawkins, 1980). The proportion engaged in twilight shifts also declined slightly during this period (from 7 to 5 per cent). It is important to recognize, however, that these changes in proportions took place at a time of an overall increase in shiftworking; hence absolute numbers working some systems may have increased even though proportionately certain systems declined.

Why has Shiftworking Increased?

Several arguments have been put forward to explain the increase in shiftworking; these include *economic* reasons, relating for example to capital utilization issues and efforts to reduce dependency on overtime working, *technical* reasons, such as the growth in continuous process industries, and *social* reasons, including the development of more continuous services to the general population. Among the strongest of these arguments appears to be employers' concern with greater capital utilization. This argument holds that as the level of capital intensity has increased, so too has the economic incentives to increase the usage from the capital by extending the hours over which it operates. Linked to this is the point that as the rate of technological change accelerates, the time scale or technological obsolescence shortens, creating a heightened desire (particularly in capital-intensive industries) to maximize the use of the technology in the short term (Bosworth *et al.*, 1981).

The extension of continuous operations, such as in steel-making and in the paper and chemical industries, necessitates round-the-clock working, not only because of the nature of the processes but also because the costs (and time) involved in shutting down and restarting operations are prohibitive. This link between continuous production and shiftworking is not a simple one, however. The level of automation in some continuous processes (such as in the chemical industry), as well as extending the hours of production, has also reduced the number of workers required to perform individual operations. We shall return to the question of automation and its relationship with night work, below.

In Britain and elsewhere the causes of overtime working are in part similar to those which have given rise to increased shiftwork (e.g. to achieve a higher degree of capital utilization). If the overtime being worked is regular and for largely predictable reasons — such as meeting production targets — it may be more cost-effective for management to replace the overtime with a shift system. Whilst overtime premia tend to be between 25 per cent and 100 per cent above normal rates, it has been estimated that, on average, hourly earnings of male shift workers in manual occupations are around 17 per cent higher than their counterparts in similar occupations on day-work (Fudge, 1980, p. 1121; see also below).

As to explaining the growing amounts of shiftwork in the service sector, a significant factor is the range of services which are now offered to the public over a progressively longer portion of the 24-hour period. Fire services, energy supply, telephone exchanges and the health service have traditionally fallen into this category, and these have now been joined by shops extending their trading hours and the growth in the restaurant and other consumption and leisure-related industries. The increase in shiftwork among non-manual workers is linked in part to this growth in the service sector, though certain new occupations, such as computer technicians, are also relevant to explaining this trend, together with the increasing need for non-manual co-ordination (e.g. by production managers) of the larger number of manual workers engaged on shiftwork.

Payment for Shiftwork. Whilst the economic and technical arguments locate employers' main interest in shiftwork, the main benefit for the individual worker is that earnings are normally higher than for comparable work carried out during the normal day. Indeed, the access to extra pay together with more free time have been identified in a number of studies as primary influences on the (positive) attitudes of shiftworkers towards shiftwork. In effect this additional payment represents an acknowledgement by employers that shiftwork is disruptive and that the disruption needs to be compensated. As noted above, one estimate of average shift premia in Britain is 17 per cent of earnings. Looking at this in more detail, Bosworth and Dawkins (1981) calculated that in 1977, average shift premia ranged from just over 13 per cent (for those on the early shift of a double day pattern) to over 25 per cent (for those on permanent nights). These authors also calculate that the various premia rose by between 13 and 38 per cent over the period 1964–77.

A number of other countries maintain similar compensation levels to those operating in Britain. In the Netherlands, for example, shift premia represents an additional 10–33 per cent of wages, depending on the type of shift worked, whilst in Luxembourg the corresponding range is 15–25 per cent. In France, too, premia for shiftwork can add 25 per cent to wages (ETUI, 1979; Carpentier and Cazamian, 1977). Elsewhere, this financial compensation for working shifts is further extended by additional time off. In Denmark, for example, two hours of holiday are accrued for each week of afternoon or night shifts worked, whilst in Germany a number of collective agreements specify two or three additional days holiday for shiftworkers (ETUI, 1979).

Yet whilst shiftwork has increased over the last three decades, with the supply of shiftworking being secured by improved compensation, it is far less clear to what extent this represents a *progressive* step in work patterns, particularly given the health and social implications of certain aspects of shiftwork.

Shiftworking and Individual Well-being

Most people used to daytime working would greet the prospect of working night shifts with some alarm. Being at work when the rest of one's family, and the majority of fellow citizens, are asleep in bed, and then trying to sleep when the rest of the community is up, about and making a noise, offers few compensations other than a financial one. Indeed, a substantial body of research exists which catalogues the social, psychological and medical problems which tend to be associated with shiftwork. This research dates back many years, and in part stems from wartime concerns with the effects of additional shiftworking. The Factory Acts of the nineteenth century which prohibited women and young people from working at night are an earlier acknowledgement of the hazards of shiftworking.

In reviewing studies of shiftwork and health, Mann (1965) identifies a number of contradictory findings, though in terms of basic functions such as sleep and digestion, he concludes that 'there is a consensus that shiftwork disrupts the time-oriented body functions of a sizeable proportion of workers' (p. 116). In their own study of over a thousand shift workers, Mann and his colleagues (Mott *et al.*, 1965) found supporting evidence for this statement, though no clear evidence of any link with more serious health complaints such as ulcers — a relationship which had been identified in earlier European studies (e.g. Thiis-Evensen, 1958, and Pierach, cited in Mann, 1965).

It is clear that of the different shifts, nightwork gives rise to the most serious problems. Whilst morning and afternoon shifts may create inconvenience, it is night-working which impacts most upon the circadian rhythms (or biological 'clocks') which govern the human metabolism. Under this rhythm the body becomes more active during the day (for example a higher body temperature, pulse, brain activity, breath rhythm and blood pressure) and de-activates at night (Carpentier and Cazamian, 1977; Wilkinson, 1978). Whilst researchers disagree on the length of time needed for the body to adapt to an inversion of patterns of day and night activity, there is some consensus that (i) this period may be quite considerable (Wilkinson, for example, notes that adaptation after three weeks is only partial), and full adaptation may not be possible; (ii) rotation of shifts from day to day or week to week hinders or prevents adaptation, as do 'rest days' which involve a temporary return to normal diurnal rountines. Further, the relationship of night-shift working to the circadian rhythm is double-edged, for not only is the individual required to be active at night, but he also has to sleep during the day, when many bodily functions are more active which, in conjunction with other factors such as the level of daytime noise, tends to make for sleep of an inferior quality.

The health drawbacks of night work are potentially compounded by additional disturbances to domestic and social life. In the family, night work affects both the practical organization of domestic life and the quality of relations within the family. In terms of the former, the night worker must choose whether to conform to his family's routine (such as eating times) or follow a routine independent of the other members of the family (a second alternative of having the family follow the night-worker's routine is only really possible in a minority of cases, such as where there are no children in the family, or where the spouse also works at night). Moreover, in a family with young children, maintaining a quiet house during the day can give rise to considerable problems, particularly in low quality housing which is poorly sound insulated (Thiis-Evensen, 1958). As for family relations, shiftwork may affect not only the amount of time members spend with one another, but also the satisfactory performance of roles within the family. Different shifts are likely to have a differential impact on domestic relations. Mott *et al.* (1965), for example, found that afternoon shifts impacted most upon individuals' roles as *parents* (by being absent during the late afternoon/early evening period), whereas night shifts restricted *marital* roles. At the same time those shift arrangements which contain additional time off, compared to daytime workers, may alleviate such problems, to a greater or lesser extent.

Broader social and psychological problems have also been associated with shiftworking in general, and nightwork in particular. In part these problems may be seen to stem from the isolating effect of what Carpentier and Cazamian (1977) term the 'de-synchronisation of leisure times' between shift and other workers, and the way public transport systems, forms of entertainment, etc., mirror a daytime working society rather than a round-the-clock one. This 'outsideness' may also be mirrored in aspects of the work organization. For whilst shift crews tend to form more cohesive workgroups compared to their daytime colleagues (due perhaps to their shared experience of working unsocial hours), a feeling of enstrangement from management, the union and the rest of the workforce is possible, if not likely. Given that most managers, for example, work only the daytime hours, this will potentially reduce not only the quality of communication between management and those working on the night shift, but could also circumscribe the degree of involvement in decision-making which those working at night could achieve. At the same time this lack of involvement may be at least partially counterbalanced by the greater discretion which the night worker typically enjoys due to lower levels of supervision at night (Carpentier and Cazamian, 1977).

Recent Developments in Shiftwork Arrangements

The previous sections, indicating the increasing use of shiftwork and its possible health and social implications (particularly of night working), provide the background against which to examine certain recent innovations in shiftworking practices. Few of the developments taking place are occurring on any large scale, at least not in Britain; indeed, one study has commented that shiftwork innovations are 'not a live issue in the UK' (Institute of Manpower Studies, 1981). This is an overgeneralization, but it remains true that innovations in this area, like many other aspects of working time, are occurring only gradually and within individual companies rather than across whole industries and sectors. Nevertheless, a number of useful points can be drawn from the developments which have occurred, and three areas of innovation in particular which echo themes raised in other chapters are the introduction of five crew working in continuous shiftwork operations, the increasing flexibility of shiftwork arrangements, and the provisions made for older workers.

Much continuous shiftwork takes the form of a four crew pattern; at any one time three crews are working and the fourth is enjoying a rest day. Often these crews will work an average 42 hour week (168 total weekly hours ÷ 4 = 42 hours). Given that many industries now operate a standard 38 to 40 hours, the four crew system thus has built into it a substantial degree of overtime. A major attraction to employers of introducing a fifth crew is that it potentially reduces overtime considerably, via an increase in the overall level of manpower. This five crew pattern has existed in some firms for many years, though it is only in recent years that interest has grown and closer attention been paid to it. Given its effect of reducing working hours and increasing levels of employment, it is not surprising that the idea of five crew working has found favour in a number of trade union circles in recent years. Both international and national union federations, including the United Federation of Italian Unions and the French CFDT, have supported the idea, indicating various possible benefits.

Employers never fail to stress how costly these measures [the

introduction of a fifth shift crew] will be, but the CFDT estimates that sufficient account is not being taken of the effects on
direct costs to the employer of absenteeism and accidents at
work, and on the population at large of unemployment and
social security (CFDT, quoted in ETUI, 1980, p. 51).

In Britain, a number of individual unions have also expressed
interest in five crew working (see, for example, GMWU, 1979).
Whilst during the recent period of widespread manpower reductions the growth of five crew working has been limited (more so in
Britain than certain other countries such as in Scandinavia) a small
number of recent case studies of five crew working do exist. One
such, by Rathkey (1984) underlines a number of the possible advantages of this practice, both for management and workforce. When
introduced into a British branch of an American owned multi-
national, Rathkey found the five crew system resulted in a halving
of the overtime worked, together with lower absenteeism and accident rates, and higher productivity. In terms of the workforce, the
new system resulted in an expansion of the number of jobs, a
reduction in weekly hours and additional days off, though among
the existing workforce these advantages were seen to be partially
offset by a reduction in the possibilities for increasing earnings via
overtime working. This picture is consistent with the findings of an
earlier study of five crew working by McEwan Young (1981), which
again pointed to advantages such as better cover, reduced absenteeism and additional time off. A previous study in the Netherlands
(Voogd, 1978), where shiftwork is generally lower than elsewhere in
Europe, found that when a five crew system was introduced in two
enterprises, one outcome was a greater willingness among workers
to work shifts.

Just as there are indications that shift patterns are capable of a
wide measure of change, so too there appears to be more scope
than has typically been recognized for introducing a measure of
flexibility into individual shiftwork patterns. The obstacles facing
this development are clear enough: in many shiftworking situations
the job must be handed over from one shift to the next, with no gap
in between. Hence any variation in individual start and stop times
must be known by corresponding workers on earlier/later shifts so
that continuity can be maintained. Nevertheless, in one of several
studies on flexitime, McEwan Young (1978) has indicated the possibilities for extending flexibility into shiftworking. As this writer

notes, *ad hoc* flexibility has long existed in individual situations with workers practising flexible handover times. With the support of management and supervisors, this arrangement can act as the basis of a broader 'personal flexibility' arrangement. This may involve a more formalized transaction system of employees indicating a desired change of start/stop time, and responding to the offers of other workers. At their most sophisticated such schemes are capable of incorporating the same debiting and crediting of hours which characterize other flexitime systems (see Chapter 7).

One of the issues raised in Chapter 8 concerning older workers relates to the potential advantages accruing to the practice of enabling those approaching retirement gradually to reduce their work hours and/or job responsibilities. Given the possible health and social costs attached to some forms of shiftwork, it is important to consider ways in which shiftwork arrangements may reflect the particular needs of older workers. The most straightforward of these would be the provision for older workers to have the right to transfer to daywork at a certain age. This already occurs on an *ad hoc* basis in many situations; proportionately more shiftwork is undertaken by men with young families, compared to their younger or older counterparts (here again the importance of the enhanced pay associated with shiftwork is evident).

It is in France where the provision for older workers to transfer from shifts to day work has been most formalized. Casey and Bruche (1983), for example, have noted a number of collective agreements which guarantee workers aged above 55 the right to transfer to day work (in some cases, provided a minimum period has been worked on shifts in the past; in the oil processing and chemical industries this period is as high as 20 years). In addition a number of these agreements provide for partial income maintenance to compensate for any reduction in earnings resulting from the loss of shift premia (Casey and Bruche, 1983, p. 8).

Conclusions

Given the patterning of time in industrial societies generally, as an aspect of the design of working time, shiftwork is, at best, a mixed blessing. On the one hand, shiftwork fulfils various economic and technical objectives, and at the same time appeals to some groups in the workforce primarily for the enhanced earnings it yields. On the other hand, the evidence suggests that associated health and social costs may be considerable particularly in relation to night-work, which breaks the biological law that human beings function best by being active during the day and asleep at night.

The indications are, however, that health and other drawbacks notwithstanding, shiftwork is unlikely to decline in the foreseeable future, despite the development of more automated processes and the contraction of certain industries where shiftwork has tradi-tionally been high (for example the coal and steel industries). For at a time of growing capital intensity, increased continuous processes and an accelerating pace of technical obsolescence, the economic and technical arguments favouring shiftwork are likely to outweigh any counter health and social factors. Furthermore, there is an argument that says shiftworking should be encouraged to expand as a means of creating additional employment. Hughes (1978b), for example, has argued that increasing shiftworking in those parts of manufacturing where it is currently at a low level, would offer a sizeable increase in employment, without requiring much change to the level of capital stock. The perceived advantage of this means of job creation over the alternative of large amounts of capital investment, is that in many contexts this latter approach would at best require very large amounts of capital input, and at worst carries the risk of having a greater job-displacing than job-creating effect.

If shiftworking is to continue increasing, it is all the more impor-tant to consider in what ways current shift patterns may be modi-fied to mitigate some of the more pressing problems. Some of these have already been mentioned in the foregoing discussion — examining ways of increasing the individual's flexibility over shift start-up and stop times, for example, or reducing the number of hours worked by those on shifts by introducing an extra crew.

As we have indicated, however, the problems associated with shiftwork are most evident in relation to nightwork, and a number of calls have been made both by international labour organizations and within individual countries, for the reduction of nightworking. In France, for example, the *Wisner Report* in 1976 called for a systematic reduction in nightwork, in part by increasing efforts to substitute automated processes at night. Subsequently the French government has imposed certain restrictions on new shiftwork arrangements (though not on existing systems), as well as laying down requirements for periodic medical examinations for shift-workers (Bosworth and Dawkins, 1978, p. 33). In this respect, the trend in Britain between 1964 and 1978 towards a smaller proportion of shiftworkers involved in nightwork is encouraging; however, given the rise in the total number involved in shiftworking, the *absolute* numbers involved in nightworking, far from falling, probably increased over that period.

If one of the main problems for nightworkers is fatigue associated with a poor sleep pattern, a shorter shift or the provision of more rest periods during the shift could act to alleviate this problem, at least to some extent. This may also be justified on productivity grounds given the finding that worker productivity tends to be considerably lower when on nightwork, compared to the other shifts (Wilkinson, 1978).

Shift patterns not involving a night shift appear to contain far fewer health problems, though for domestic and social reasons the morning or 'day' shift tends to be far more popular than 'afternoons' (for this reason, Wilkinson among others has advocated the rapid rotation of morning and afternoon shifts to minimize the build up of dissatisfaction among afternoon shiftworkers). The unpopularity of particular shifts may be further alleviated by mixing periods of shiftwork with periods of normal day working, thereby potentially easing any isolating effects the shift worker may experience *vis-à-vis* the family, community and work organization.

The question of the most suitable rate of rotation of continuous shifts is a complex one. On the one hand, there is the argument that for the body to adjust to night working the rotation should be infrequent; indeed, most successful adjustment would be created by having no rotation at all (Walker, 1970; Wilkinson, 1978). Yet whilst a slow rotation (or none at all) may be preferable from a biological point of view, from a social and domestic standpoint, a fast rotation may be preferable, thus preventing the hardships accruing to particular shifts from becoming overbearing (though at the cost of additional fatigue and absence of biological adjustment to any particular shift).

Recent innovations have suggested that shiftwork systems may be capable of far greater flexibility than had previously been thought. Given the prospects for continued growth of shiftworking, this aspect of working time warrants closer investigation, on the merits of different shiftwork systems (particularly those avoiding nightworking), and the nature of employee preferences (for example, towards a slow versus fast rotation of shifts under a double day system). More generally, however, greater enquiry is required into the way society, and particularly certain aspects within it (housing, transport, trading hours, entertainment, etc.), can be modified to reflect more satisfactorily a community in which a sizeable and growing minority are working outside the normal daytime hours.

Notes

1. Another possible means of reducing overtime which has received some attention is that of increasing overtime premia, as a means of discouraging employers from resorting to its use (see Ehrenberg and Schumann, 1982). At present, however, there appears to be relatively little support for this idea, particularly on this side of the Atlantic.

2. NES data tends to underestimate the total volume of shiftworking, however, since it counts only full-time workers, and in particular those full-timers receiving shift premia in the specific reference period of the survey.

3. This may also be categorized as a 'semi-continuous' system, with 'discontinuous' being used to describe those systems where the total duration of daily activity is less than 24 hours, as under Double Day arrangements (see, for example, ILO, 1978, p. 18).

4 HOLIDAYS

Holidays with pay have been one of labour's great gains in the last few decades (Evans, 1969).

Whilst much of the discussion on working time has focused on aspects of the working week (weekly hours, part-time working, etc.) and the working lifetime (retirement practices, school-leaving ages, etc.), the past decade has witnessed significant changes in the working *year*, resulting from increases in paid holiday entitlement. By 1981, almost nine out of ten full-time adult men in Britain had annual holiday entitlement of four weeks or more; in 1970 the proportion had been just two in every ten. Elsewhere, a similar growth in holiday entitlement has been witnessed; the European Trade Union Confederation's objective of six weeks annual paid holiday (ETUI, 1979) has already been reached by a growing number of occupational groups and could well be achieved by a majority of industrialized workforces in the next decade or so.

Yet, whilst the extent of holiday entitlement has increased, in a number of respects the degree of flexibility over the taking of holidays remains limited, with restricted choice over how holiday time may be organized. Before addressing this issue, however, and related questions such as the value of sabbatical leave for both the individual and the work organization, it is necessary to review some of the changes which have been occurring in holiday entitlement in Britain and abroad.

The Growth of Holidays

Developments in Britain

Like the length of the working day, the number of holidays appear to have fluctuated at different periods in history. Precise early patterns are difficult to determine, partly because rural occupations had a different pattern to their urban counterparts, and also because some artisans would break from one job at particular times in order to undertake other tasks (e.g. harvesting). Informal holidays due to absenteeism and enforced idleness resulting from lack of work further complicate the picture, as does the tendency for some groups of self-employed workers to alternate their activity between days of intensive work and days of 'playing' when no work was performed (Thompson, 1967).

Due to these many sources of variation, together with the lack of systematic data, it is not surprising that economic historians differ widely in their views on the pattern of holidays in pre-industrial Britain. Rogers (1906, p. 181), for example, argues that the picture of the medieval English labourer enjoying many holidays for religious festivities, is inaccurate; five holiday days a year (in addition to Sundays) is judged to be a more accurate figure. Bienefeld (1972), on the other hand, suggests a considerably higher figure, particularly in the fifteenth century; masons for example are noted as having holidays ranging between 20 and 27 days per annum in the fourteenth century, and as much as 46 days by the mid-fifteenth century.

According to Bienefeld, public holidays subsequently suffered a reversal under the Puritans such that, 'by the end of the seventeenth century the majority of working men enjoyed but a very few holidays around Christmas, Easter and Whitsun' (Bienefeld, 1972, p. 19). This situation is thought to have prevailed throughout the eighteenth and into the nineteenth century; in the textile mills at the beginning of the nineteenth century, for example, holidays varied from five to twelve days per year (p. 39). Further, in some areas production 'lost' through holidays had to be made up by longer hours beforehand or subsequently. Payment for holidays was almost non-existent, though by the nineteenth century, Christmas Day (in Scotland, New Year's Day) tended to be paid. Renewed enthusiasm for holidays came with rising prosperity in the 1850s. The greater access to cheap excursions on the rapidly growing railway network may have been one cause (as well as an effect) of the renewed interest in holidays.

Yet in subsequent decades the development of paid holidays increased only very slowly, both in Britain and abroad. By 1936, only about one and a half million workers in the UK had agreements providing holidays with pay (Evans, 1969, p. 50). By the mid-1950s, paid holiday entitlement had become widespread, though remained restricted in length — paid holidays of less than two weeks was the norm for almost all manual workers in Britain (Trade Union Research Unit, 1981). This level persisted until 1960

Table 4.1: Changes in Holiday Entitlement in Britain, 1970–1981

% of employees with holiday entitlement of:	Men				Women			
	Manual		Non-manual		Manual		Non-manual	
Weeks	1970	1981	1970	1981	1970	1981	1970	1981
0/1/2	15	2	4	2	15	3	9	2
+2, <4	78	11	47	8	80	20	60	10
4	3	26	18	22	2	29	8	30
+4–5	3	51	17	41	2	42	9	37
+5	1	11	14	28	1	6	15	21

Source: Department of Employment, 'Pattern of holiday entitlement', *Employment Gazette*, Vol. 89, No. 12, Dec. 1981, p. 534.

and only modestly increased during the following decade; by 1969, average paid holiday entitlement for manual workers was 2.3 weeks.

A much greater rate of change characterized the 1970s and early 80s, however, and as the overall level of holiday entitlement increased, some narrowing of differentials took place in Britain between the holidays afforded to manual and non-manual workers (Table 4.1). In 1970 almost half the non-manual men in Britain had holiday entitlement of four weeks or more, compared to less than one in ten of male manual workers; by 1981 the corresponding proportions were 90 per cent, compared with 87 per cent. The gap between the holiday entitlement of manual and non-manual women also narrowed, as did that between men and women overall. Yet Table 4.1 shows, despite these developments, considerable disparity between the groups was still evident in 1981, particularly in relation to access to more than five weeks holiday per annum.

More recently the trend beyond four weeks has continued, though at a slower rate. By the end of 1983, average holiday entitlement of manual workers in Britain had risen to 21¾ days; 95 per cent of manual workers enjoyed a minimum of four weeks holiday, and nearly a fifth had entitlement of five weeks or more (Department of Employment, 1984). Analysis of collective agreements shows a similar pattern. The TUC, for example, noted a total of 121 collective agreements between February 1982 and February 1983 which improved basic leave beyond four weeks; forty four of the agreements increased the basic leave to at least five weeks (25 days) and a further 38 agreements brought holiday entitlement to within one or two days of five weeks (TUC, 1983a, 1983b and 1983c). When account is taken of the extra days given for long service, (over one-third of manual workers benefit from extra service entitlements) the picture in Britain appears to be one where the pattern of holiday entitlement is much nearer to attaining that called for by the TUC and ETUC (6 weeks annual holiday), than appears the case for other aspects of working time, in particular the 35 hour week for all workers and retirement at 60 years.

Developments outside Britain

As in Britian, the development of paid holidays in most other industrial countries is a relatively recent phenomenon. In the late 1920s, holidays with pay appear to have been rare, though not altogether absent. Certain privileged groups of workers (e.g. state and local authority officials, senior and professional grade employees), enjoyed paid holiday at this time, and in a number of countries (including Austria, Finland, Poland and the USSR), general regulations providing holidays with pay (usually six days) had been created between 1919 and 1922 (Evans, 1969, p. 50). By 1934, however, there were only 12 countries with holiday legislation; the minimum duration of annual leave was four days in three of these countries, one week in six others and two weeks in the other three (ILO, 1984, p. 90). By 1938, most European countries had enacted legislation on paid holidays, usually providing for one week per annum.

Subsequently, this level was extended in Europe, broadly in line with developments in Britain; however, a notable difference continues to be the greater role of legislation laying down minimum holiday entitlement in many countries outside Britain (Table 4.2). In a number of countries collective agreements between employers and unions follow the legislation, though in others the agreements have improved on the levels of statutory minimum leave.

It is evident that the minimum holiday entitlement, either as defined by legislation or collective agreement, is four weeks. In a majority of countries, the legislation was extended during the 1970s and early 80s to four, or in some cases five, weeks (ETUI, 1979). In a number of cases this leave entitlement has been extended further in subsequent years. In Austria, for example, legislation in 1982 and 1983 made provision for an extra week's holiday to be achieved in stages by 1986 (ETUI, 1984, p. 80). Holiday increases were also achieved in the Federal Republic of Germany during 1983 with

Table 4.2: Paid Annual Leave and Public Holidays in Western Europe

Country	Basic annual leave as determined by		Number of Public Holidays
	(i) Law	(ii) Collective agreement (average levels)	
Austria	4 weeks, 2 days	cf. Law	13
Belgium	4 weeks	4 to 5 weeks	10
Denmark	—	5 weeks	9½
Fed. Rep. Germany	3 weeks	4 to 6 weeks	9–13
Finland	5 weeks	5 to 6 weeks	5
France	5 weeks	5 to 6 weeks	6–9
Greece	4 weeks	cf. Law	6–12
Iceland	4 weeks, 4 days	cf. Law	?
Ireland	3 weeks	4 weeks	7
Italy	—	4 to 6 weeks	10–11
Luxembourg	5 weeks	cf. Law	10
Malta	4 weeks	cf. Law	6
Netherlands	3 weeks	4 to 5 weeks	7
Norway	4 weeks, 1 day	cf. Law	10
Portugal	4 weeks	cf. Law	?
Spain	5 weeks	5 weeks	14
Sweden	5 weeks	5 to 8 weeks	11
Switzerland	4 weeks	4 to 5 weeks	8
United Kingdom	—	4 to 6 weeks	8–10

Source: European Trade Union Institute, *Reduction of Working Hours in Western Europe*, Part 1, Brussels, 1979; European Trade Union Institute, *Collective Bargaining in Western Europe in 1983 and Prospects for 1984*, Brussels, 1984.

the result that at the end of that year 96 per cent of workers in Germany were entitled to at least four weeks leave per year, 86 per cent to five weeks or more, and 47 per cent to six weeks (ibid.). Likewise, following agreements reached in Spain during 1983, more than 95 per cent of workers enjoy five weeks annual leave. In Switzerland, where the law covering minimum annual leave was extended from two to four weeks in December 1983, the trade union federation (the SGB) has subsequently pursued a policy of five weeks leave for workers over 40 years.[1]

Additionally, in many countries provision for extra holiday entitlement is made mainly on length of service but occasionally on age (e.g. in Germany, Norway and if the union claim is successful, in Switzerland). In Norway, for example, those over 60 years are entitled to an extra week's holiday above the statutory minimum. Furthermore, particular groups (e.g. handicapped workers) in

Germany and Luxembourg, and employed mothers with young children in France, together with those working in particular sectors of industry, also have longer holidays. Other variations between countries (and between regions within the same country) occur due to differences in the number of public holidays, which are additional to legal or collectively agreed holiday entitlement (see Table 4.2).

The pattern of paid holidays in the United States stands in marked contrast to the developments in Europe. In 1979 the average length of paid holidays in the US was just two weeks, only a slight rise from the 1.9 weeks average prevailing in 1968 (Hedges and Taylor, 1980). For a small minority of long-service workers this vacation is extended by occasional long-service leave (see discussion on sabbaticals, below). Hedges and Taylor (1980, p. 9) note that the growth in paid vacation has not kept pace with demand, evidenced for example by the significant increase between 1968 and 1979 of employees taking extra unpaid holidays.

In Japan, too, the pattern of holidays is considerably different to that in Europe. Kotaro (1980) notes that annual holidays in Japan have not kept pace with changing international standards. Total holiday time in Japan is further reduced by the common practice of employees not using their full allocation of holiday (p. 68) but instead to work part of their holiday to increase income. Another peculiarity of holiday patterns in Japan is the tendency for Japanese workers not to take long vacations, but to take short periods of holiday, usually just one or two days (Hanami, 1980, p. 161).

Overall, the picture seems to be one of holiday entitlement extending considerably in quantitative terms during the 1970s and early 80s. This extra holiday entitlement represents a noticeable reduction in working time — five days extra holiday per year is not only equivalent to an hour off the working week but is also packaged in a way that allows more leisure utility to be gained from the free time. As White (1980) has commented, it is surprising that compared to the question of reduced weekly hours, holiday increases have not attracted similar attention. This may reflect not only the fact that until recently the amount of paid holiday was relatively small but also that increases have tended to be introduced in small increments. However, the major increase in holiday entitlement during the last decade suggests that this aspect of working time (and its relationship to, for example, labour turnover, absenteeism, employee preferences over work time and particularly the level of employment[2]) warrants closer attention.

Qualitative Aspects of Holiday Entitlement

Whilst recent advances in the quantitative aspects of holidays are clear, developments in the *qualitative* aspects of holidays are much less evident. One of the important qualitative aspects of holidays has already been touched upon — the growth of *paid* holidays. Payment may be less for holiday periods than for weeks that are worked, due to holidays reflecting basic pay rather than average earnings, or — as is the case in some countries — a result of holidays being paid at a rate which is a proportion of earnings (ETUI, 1984, p. 89). Nevertheless, payment for holidays has enhanced their value considerably, and not only removed (or at least mitigated) the cost of respite from work routines but also increased the possibilities of holidays being spent on excursions away from home.

Yet other qualitative aspects of holiday entitlement have not increased at the same rate as the overall level of annual leave. Indeed, holiday patterns continue to reflect considerable degrees of inflexibility which together impose a significant restriction on many workers' ability to construct their preferred worktime/holiday pattern. Principally, this inflexibility stems from restrictions over when holidays may be taken. In many production industries, for example, a significant part of the annual leave must be taken at certain times, during which the plant is shut down. In the British iron and steel industry, for example, these shut-down or 'stop' weeks tend to occur towards the end of July and beginning of August. Additionally, the period from before Christmas to after the New Year has increasingly become a second period of shut-down. As a result, a considerable proportion of workers, disproportionately those in blue-collar grades, have discretion over only a part of their annual leave entitlement.

During the 1970s in Britain, the extension of leave entitlement was accompanied by further restrictions on when at least part of that leave could be taken (for example, many employees gained extra leave at Christmas which was not transferable to another time, but rather was used to create a single holiday period from Christmas through to the New Year). In his study of 400 establishments in five manufacturing industries (food, chemicals, mechanical and electrical engineering and clothing/footwear), White (1980) found that 45 per cent of establishments operated at least one shutdown period longer than five days. For employers this provides not only more certainty of production (compared to a situation where workers are taking holidays at different times), but also allows for a concentrated period of plant maintenance. In the iron and steel industry, for example, stop weeks are used for repairs to, and relining of, furnaces. As a result, total overtime requirements to carry out maintenance work are reduced; White found that those establishments who operated a shut-down period worked, on average, 25 per cent less overtime than those without a shut-down.

Similar restrictions on choice are also evident outside Britain. In the Netherlands, for example, regulations exist which require annual leave in the main industrial and commercial sectors to begin on one of three different dates, separated by two week intervals (Haulot, 1979, p. 193). Belgium, France and Italy also have traditional close-down periods in July (in Belgium) and August (France and Italy). In some East European countries, including Czechoslovakia and Romania, a much greater degree of staggering of holidays has been developed, though the extent to which the individual has discretion over the timing of holidays is unclear (Haulot, 1979, pp. 193, 200).

Whilst for many employees shut-down weeks limit the degree of choice over when leave can be taken, for an even larger proportion of working people this discretion is further inhibited by the requirement that all leave must be taken within a twelve month period. At most, only a limited 'carry over' of holiday entitlement is allowed and for the majority this option would seem to be absent. One effect of this is to restrict the possibility of 'banking' unused holiday in order to engage in lengthier pursuits such as extended foreign travel. Again little information is available on this aspect of working time, though the picture would seem to be one of only a few (usually white-collar) groups being afforded a degree of carry over. For the rest, the lack of this facility often leads to the taking of unwanted holidays at unpopular times (in Britain typically this is in March), as a result of having held some leave days unused as cover for unforeseen emergencies.

Certain notable exceptions to this practice do exist, however. For example, the French Peugeot-Citroen car company introduced a scheme in the 1970s which enabled employees in its 180 plants to accumulate leave credits on the basis of their working conditions, age and attendance records, which could then be translated in the short term into longer holidays, or in the longer term into periods of sabbatical leave, or even earlier retirement (Tavernier, 1978). There is little indication at the present time, however, that such examples of more flexible leave arrangements are poised to become commonplace.

Sabbaticals

The concept of sabbatical leave attracted considerable attention in the 1960s and 70s, due mainly to the idea that a period away from the job doing something different (particularly some form of education) would help managers return to their jobs 'refreshed and refueled' (Dickson, 1975, p. 260). The idea was not a new one; many academic institutions, for example, have long accepted the sabbatical as a vehicle for staff to conduct research, gain new ideas and wider insight. By the early 1970s there is some evidence of a growing interest in sabbaticals particularly in US industry. One poll in the United States at that time, involving over 200 companies, found that almost one quarter had a programme which they considered to be a sabbatical; generally this involved leave for middle managers to engage in some form of education or training (Dickson, 1975, p. 262). In addition, extended vacations, usually from 10 to 13 weeks, are available periodically to some long service employees in the United States. Hedges and Taylor (1980) note that about 5 per cent of all collective bargaining agreements in 1976 included provision for extended vacations. In part this provision reflects the generally lower level of paid vacation in the United States, compared to many other countries (see above).

In Britain support for a greater availability of sabbatical leave has come from various quarters, including Jenkins and Sherman (1979) who advocate sabbaticals as part of a broader strategy to reduce worktime in response to technological change; their suggestion is that each employee should have the right to four year-long sabbaticals during a working lifetime. A similar idea was put forward by the Work in America research group in the early 1970s, recommending one six month educational sabbatical every seven years (or one year every 14 years); this was seen as a means of making lifelong education a reality, the costs involved being offset by greater productivity, a reduction in unemployment and a reorganization of existing *ad hoc* training programmes (Dickson, 1975, pp. 264–5).

For the foreseeable future, however, access to sabbatical leave is likely to remain highly restricted and the preserve of aspiring and established managers in medium or large companies, and a small number of professions. The costs involved, and the problems for smaller companies of individuals being absent for long periods, will act as a forceful brake on any extension of the sabbatical concept. In identifying this widespread lack of commitment to meeting the costs of such schemes, Rathkey (1984) suggests that a more practical approach to the question of sabbaticals would be to extend the principle of greater leave entitlement for longer service workers, e.g. an additional two weeks leave every seventh year of service. On a limited scale, longer holidays for longer serving employees already exists. However, one widely publicised scheme which operates more on the scale that Rathkey suggests involves US steelworkers who negotiated an agreement back in 1963 providing senior production workers with a period of 13 weeks extra leave for every five years worked (Dickson, 1975, p. 263). Overall, however, it seems unlikely that extended holidays and sabbaticals will become widely available for most blue- and white-collar grades in the immediate future. Time off to attend educational courses may become more common for some managerial and technical groups (for example, those most affected by changes in information technology developments), though this need is likely to be catered for more by short intensive courses and part-time attendance, rather than by lengthy sabbaticals.

Unpaid or Part-paid Leave

One option which could become more readily available in coming years is the facility for taking unpaid or part-paid leave. The extent to which this is already available is not clear. White (1980) in a preliminary study found that 'virtually every firm was prepared to permit extra holiday without pay under some circumstances' (p. 27). However, it would appear that in many work organizations these 'circumstances' are highly restricted. Further, given the time taken to establish payment for holidays, some would see a greater availability of unpaid leave as a dangerous precedent, potentially inhibiting the further extension of paid holidays. Yet the choice to extend paid holiday with extra unpaid leave would increase a worker's ability to trade income for additional non-work time. For the employer, offering leave of absence to employees could have some of the 'rejuvenating' effects of sabbaticals, whilst at the same time making savings on the total wage bill.

With continued pressure on public services to cut expenditure, one might foresee a leave of absence provision being particularly relevant within local and central government and public services. Such a scheme would be fairly easy to administer, with agreed maxima of unpaid leave, along with agreed protection of, for example, contracts of employment, job continuity, etc. Here again, though, the potential social divisiveness of worktime is apparent, with higher income, non-manual households likely to be far more capable of taking advantage of an unpaid leave facility than lower wage earners. However, if adequate protection was also extended to subsequent pension entitlement, this could increase the appeal of unpaid leave to a broader section of older workers whose outgoings, such as mortgage repayments, have declined.

Conclusion

Given the timescale involved in the initial development of paid holidays, their growth in the 1970s appears even more remarkable. Though the signs are that this growth has slowed, some further increase in coming years may be expected as management respond to demands for shorter working time. For in many respects, managements are likely to regard extending holiday entitlement as preferable to cutting the working week. In part this reflects the smaller reduction in total hours likely to be involved in a settlement involving holidays rather than weekly hours. Additionally, if management imposed restrictions on the timing of any extra leave, this could allow holidays to be grouped into slack work periods (as, for example, in the recent extensions of holidays around Christmas). Moreover, since the managerial practice of work groups 'covering' for individuals on holiday is well-established in many work organizations, even where discretion is given over timing of holidays, this could affect overall productivity less than an equivalent reduction in the working week.

A further impetus to extending holidays may also be present in the already widespread use of shut-down periods; these may generate further adoption of this practice where companies staying open, for example between Christmas and New Year, find their business severely hampered by other work organizations being closed.

For employees, too, notably for certain groups such as women with school-age children, extra periods of annual holiday are likely to be particularly well-received, since for many this represents a more useful period of non-work time than a small reduction in the working week. Yet the contribution of holidays to increasing individual discretion over worktime will only become truly significant when the flexibility of entitlement is increased by extending facilities for carry over, the longer term banking of holidays and the greater provision of sabbatical and unpaid leave. By creating sizeable periods within the working lifetime when education and other forms of experience can be acquired, this would go a long way to breaking down the rigidity of the education—work—leisure sequence, which typifies the life pattern of the majority in industrialized societies.

Notes

1. Minimum leave entitlement is on average lower in Eastern Europe; the minimum annual leave in Bulgaria and Poland is 14 days (2 weeks in Czechoslovakia), whilst in Hungary, Romania and the USSR the minimum is 15 days, rising to 18 days in the German Democratic Republic and Yugoslavia (ILO, 1984). Among 142 member states of the ILO as a whole in 1983/4 less than 10 per cent had a minimum holiday duration of less than two weeks, compared to 45 per cent with a minimum duration of at least two weeks, 20 per cent with at least three weeks and 25 per cent with at least four weeks or more (ibid., p. 90).

2. The Department of Employment (1978b) calculated that a week's extra holiday could create between 25,000 and 100,000 jobs, though at the expense of a 2 per cent increase in labour costs. In his later survey, White (1980) found that when asked to contemplate a substantial increase in holiday entitlement (10 days), managers estimated that this would result in an increased manual recruitment of 3.5 per cent (and 1.3 per cent for non-manual workers), together with a 5 per cent increase in costs.

5 SHORT-TIME WORKING

Just as overtime seeks to change the length of the productive period without altering the total number of workers employed, short-time working measures have a similar objective, but in the reverse direction — maintaining the size of the workforce during a period of slack demand by reducing the number of hours worked by some or all employees.[1] If, for example, an employer is faced with a temporary decline in demand equivalent to the output of 20 per cent of the workforce, the reduction in output might be achieved by the whole workforce working a four instead of a five day week (thereby achieving a 20 per cent reduction in total working time) rather than the alternative of making a fifth of the workforce redundant. Hence, in terms of our discussion in Chapter 2, short-time working represents an immediate and highly visible form of work-sharing albeit one with a more short-term horizon than other work-sharing proposals discussed earlier. Further, unlike the advocates of the longer-term measures, this form of work-sharing seeks to *maintain*, rather than *increase*, the level of employment.

For the employer there are a number of possible benefits (and costs) attached to pursuing a policy of short-time working, rather than a programme of redundancies followed by re-hiring once business revives. Keeping the workforce intact during slack periods, for example, is likely to reduce the risk of losing valuable skilled workers, eliminate the cost of recruiting and training when demand recovers, and avoid the cost of redundancy payments (Reid, 1982). Absenteeism could also be expected to fall if employees are experiencing periods of free time during the week. The short-time working response to periods of inadequate demand may also be more flexible than other strategies and capable of being easily reversed given an improved economic situation (Reyher *et al.*, 1980, pp. 170−1).

From a societal point of view, the use of short-time working practices rather than redundancies may also be seen to have the advantage of being a potentially more equitable distribution of the shortage of work, than is normally found in redundancy and unemployment patterns (in which unskilled workers, those newly hired, younger and older age groups, ethnic minorities and female workers, tend to be disproportionately represented). Additionally, from the individual worker's point of view the consequences of redundancy or long-term lay off — the loss in income, fringe benefits, status, etc. — are likely to be much greater than those resulting from a period of short-time working. In many of the schemes discussed below, the level of compensation for workless days is typically between half and two-thirds normal wage levels. For the worker's trade union, the benefits of short-time working include both a preservation of membership levels, and possibly a lower degree of polarization between groups represented by the union (MaCoy and Morand, 1984, p. 6).

In several countries in recent years, governments have subsidized short-time working practices in efforts to reduce the number of redundancies and stem the rise in unemployment. A number of such schemes are reviewed below; in general they have acted both to encourage employers to utilize short-time working rather than redundancies and to cushion the effects of short-time working on the income of those workers involved. At best, compensated short-time working can result in a temporary increase with only a small drop in income. More generally a compensated short-time working scheme reduces (or at least, postpones) the threat of unemployment by creating a breathing space in the process whereby a fall in demand is translated into redundancies.

Yet despite these and other claims made in favour of short-time working, together with its increased use in several countries, this aspect of working time has not avoided criticism. This has focused on the rationale underlying short-time working and also on the actual effects of compensated short-time working schemes. Central to both of these is the timescale being considered, and in particular the 'temporariness' of the downturn in demand. If the expectation is that the downturn is indeed temporary — up to six months or even a year — then the case in favour of short-time working seems strong. In the case of a prolonged recession, however, as in the case of many industries and many countries after 1979, then the argument is stronger that short-time working will act not only simply to *postpone* rather than avoid redundancies, but also that such a measure could lead to the delaying of necessary organizational decisions which in turn could further damage the viability of the enterprise and its chances of long-term survival. Hence, as it is currently envisaged, short-time working represents a strategy

Table 5.1: Short-time Working and Redundancies in Britian, 1978–1983

	Average number of manual workers on short-time work in manufacturing (000s)	Total redundancies (000s)
1978	38	173
1979	51	187
1980	279	493
1981	335	532
1982	142	398
1983	77	311

Source: *Employment Gazette*, Vol. 92, No. 4, April 1984.

suitable for relatively short fluctuations in demand, rather than drawn-out recessions. This is reflected in the pattern of usage of short-time working. In Britain, for example, short-time, working became very prominent in the years immediately after 1979 (Table 5.1). As it became clear, however, that the recession was a longer term problem (and as the conditions of government subsidies became more restricted) the number on short-time working fell, at a more rapid rate than the number of redundancies.

The Use of Short-time Working in Britain, West Germany and North America

Britain

Whilst short-time working in Britain can involve workers registering as unemployed and claiming unemployment benefit for the (whole) days they are workless, the main vehicle by which recent governments have sought to encourage short-time working rather than redundancies, has been through the Temporary Short-Time Working Compensation Scheme (TSTWCS). State subsidies of short-time working can take various forms, including enabling workers to collect welfare payments for their workless days or compensating the employer who continues to pay normal, or a proportion of normal, earnings. The TSTWCS is an example of the latter. From its inception in 1979 the scheme has applied to all employers who agree to withdraw impending redundancies affecting at least ten workers. If, for example, an employer is faced with making ten workers redundant, he can apply for compensation for 50 workless days per week, these days then being spread over a larger group by, say, 50 employees working a four rather than a five day week.

Since its introduction, the TSTWCS has suffered several reductions in its scope, affecting both the level of compensation and the period of eligibility. At its commencement in April 1979, the TSTWCS reimbursed employers to the extent of 75 per cent of normal pay (together with national insurance contributions) for workers on their workless days, for a period of up to 12 months. By July 1982 these limits had declined to a compensation level of 50 per cent for a period of up to 6 months (Metcalf, 1982, p. 57). Hence, at a time when estimates of the length of the recession were increasing, the maximum period for which short-time compensation could be received in Britain was being reduced. This is in marked contrast to developments in West Germany, discussed below.

Despite the reduced coverage of TSTWCS, and despite a slow beginning (Metcalf notes for example that the scheme cost only £24 million in its first year), interest in the scheme developed rapidly as the recession worsened during 1980 (see Table 5.1). It reached its peak of activity in March 1981 when companies were receiving compensation for over 984,000 workers on short-time. By late 1982, however, participation in the scheme had fallen to well below 100,000. During its period of major activity, the companies taking advantage of the subsidy were located almost entirely in the manufacturing sector, and in particular within metal manufacture, engineering, textiles, clothing and footwear industries — areas of the economy hit particularly severely by the recession (Table 5.2).

Several factors account for the decline from 1982 onwards in short-time working in general and in reduced take-up of the TSTWCS in particular. First, this trend is similar to that in the 1975 recession in Germany, about which Best and Mattesich (1980) have argued that short-time working is likely to be particularly favoured during the *early* stages of a downturn, when companies are not sure whether redundancies are necessary. As estimates of the timing of a revival lengthen, schemes based on a relatively short timescale are likely to lose support as they begin to appear less appropriate to the scale of the problem. Second, as deepening recession results in widespread redundancies, fewer enterprises are capable of reducing worktime further whilst still maintaining economic viability. Third, one of the conditions of the TSTWCS is that the jobs of any

Table 5.2: Temporary Short-Time Working Compensation Scheme — Total Applications Approved for Cumulative Period 1 April 1979−31 May 1982

Sic No.	Industry	Number of applications	No. of potentially redundant jobs	No. of workers sharing
6	Metal Manufacture	1705	107,760	319,922
7	Mechanical Engineering	2481	114,153	329,989
9	Electrical Engineering	926	63,547	210,287
11	Vehicles	911	114,441	400,420
12	Metal Goods not Elsewhere Specified	2456	91,376	269,001
13	Textiles	2155	101,188	256,349
15	Clothing and Footwear	1974	86,189	199,829
16	Bricks, Pottery, Glass, Cement, etc.	659	30,067	95,923
17	Timber, Furniture, etc.	890	34,088	83,645
19	Other Manufacturing Industries	650	30,599	93,704
	All Other Industries	3776	134,993	389,299
	Great Britain Total	18,583	908,401	2,648,368

Source: Department of Employment.

particular group of workers threatened by redundancy can only be supported once through the application of short-time working compensation. Hence after a certain period has elapsed, many employers may run out of potentially redundant workers who are still eligible to act as the basis of an application for the subsidy.

The British experience of subsidizing short-time working has left a number of unresolved issues, including the appropriateness of a relatively short period for which compensation is payable, the level of compensation paid and the logic behind allowing particular jobs to be 'saved' only once, as under the TSTWCS scheme. The experiences of short-time working in West Germany and North America shed some additional light on these issues, as well as on the more general question of the effectiveness and overall value of this change in working time as a response to unfavourable economic conditions.

West Germany

Some form of state subsidy of short-time working has been in operation in West Germany since 1927 — longer than in any other country. The current provisions stem from a scheme (the Kurzbar-beitergeld-Kug) established in 1969 by the Employment Promotion Act, under which allowances are paid to employees on short-time, providing that the arrangement has the agreement of the company's Works Council and that the company can show both that the work shortage is unavoidable and that the worktime reductions will prevent dismissals. The proposed short-time working must involve at least 10 per cent of the working time for one-third or more of the workforce for a minimum period of four weeks. Allowances equal to 68 per cent of loss in earnings are paid (via the employer) to employees on short-time; when tax effects are taken into account most people receiving the short-time allowance achieve more than 90 per cent of their former pay. In response to the recent recession, which was felt increasingly in Germany after 1981, the normal six month period of entitlement was extended, up to 24 months in areas with high rates of unemployment; in 1982 this was further extended to up to three years in relation to the depressed iron and steel industry (Meisel, 1984). By January 1983, some 1.2 million workers in West Germany were receiving short-time compensation payments.

As in Britain, very little short-time working occurs in Germany during periods of economic growth except in a small number of companies experiencing specific problems. Reyher *et al.* (1980) note that on average during the 1960s, there were only about 10,000 workers on short-time in any one period. After 1973, however, the extent of short-time working increased, particularly during the early stages of recession in 1975, and again in 1983 (Table 5.3).

Reyher *et al.* have estimated that in 1975, short-time working reduced the number of registered unemployed by 147,000. As in Britain, short-time working in Germany tends to be heavily concentrated in the production sector and in particular in mining, metal production and processing, mechanical engineering, the electrical industry and the textile and clothing industry (Reyher *et al.*, 1980, p. 168). In an effort to examine some of the criticisms of short-time subsidies — for example that they do not prevent redundancies but merely postpone them, and that hours lost through short-time working are made up by increased overtime — Reyher and colleagues examined the experiences of the mechanical engineering industry between 1974 and 1976 in the Baden-Wurthenberg region of West Germany (a region which is a heavy user of short-time working; see Meisel, 1984, p. 59). The results are on the whole

Table 5.3: Subsidized Short-time Working in West Germany, Selected Years 1968–1983

	Short-time workers (000s) (average)	Unemployment rate (%)
1968	10	1.3
1972	76	0.9
1974	292	2.2
1975	773	4.7
1978	191	4.2
1983 (average of 1st quarter)	1,121	10.1

Sources: F. Best and J. Mattesich, 'Short-time compensation schemes in California and Europe', *Monthly Labor Review*, July 1980, Vol. 103, No. 7, p. 18; L. Reyher, M. Koller and E. Spitznagel, *Employment Policy Alternatives to Unemployment in the Federal Republic of Germany*, Anglo-German Foundation, London 1980, p. 169; H. Meisel, 'The Pioneers: STC in the Federal Republic of Germany', in R. MaCoy and M. Morand (eds.), *Short-Time Compensation*, Pergamon Press, New York, 1984, p. 59.

favourable towards short-time working, in particular its apparent impact on redundancies, and that it was not paralleled by an increase in overtime — on the contrary, overtime was also cut back to reduce the volume of manpower.

Overall, the picture in West Germany is one of short-time compensation being used over a long period of time, and expanded to meet the conditions facing particular industries and regions suffering acutely from recession. Government support for this policy has remained strong, as voiced by a spokesman in 1976 who commented that short-time work subsidies had proved an 'effective instrument of labour market policy that can be employed rapidly on a regional, sectoral and individual enterprise basis' (from a West German Embassy publication, cited in Levitan and Belous, 1977, p. 63).

North America

The idea of compensating workers for short-time working is a recent one in North America and compared to most European countries is still far from securely established. In latter years, however, it has formed the focus of work-sharing discussion across the Atlantic (so much so that the terms short-time working and work-sharing are used synonymously in America, unlike Europe where work-sharing contains much wider connotations; see Chapter 2).

Whilst uncompensated short-time working has figured prominently in past recessions in the US, notably in the Great Depression of the 1930s (Nemirow, 1984), the development of subsidized schemes has been hindered by the inflexibility of the Unemployment Insurance (UI) laws which in practice give welfare entitlement only to those workers who are completely laid off. This has acted to discourage short-time working, although some companies have utilized 'rotation layoffs' whereby employees rotate weeks of work and non-work, thus securing UI benefits for the latter (McCarthy and Rosenberg, 1981, pp. 18–19).

In recent years this picture has begun to change, with the US government passing legislation in 1982 directing the Secretary of Labor to draw up model legislation, paving the way for individual states to adopt an amended form of UI provision which allows for compensated short-time working. The stimulus for this has come from a scheme operating in California since 1978. In 1982 amendments were also made to the Canadian UI laws to facilitate short-time working; again this followed an experimental period and subsequent evaluation.

California. In 1978 the Californian state government introduced a Work-Sharing Unemployment Insurance programme, which enabled employees working short-time to receive a weekly UI benefit proportional to the percentage reduction in wages and hours, for a maximum period of 20 weeks. Whilst initial take up was low, the scheme grew in popularity to the point where in 1982 an average of over 8,000 employees per month (and a yearly total for that year of almost 100,000) received the compensation (Lammers and Lockwood, 1984). Following legislation in 1983 (which extends the scheme up to 1986) the basic period of eligibility has been extended to 26 weeks, and up to 52 weeks if unemployment in California registers more than 7.5 per cent. Lammers and Lockwood (1984, p. 76) note that overall the scheme has meant that the average worker collecting the subsidy has maintained 92 per cent of his/her wages and fringe benefits, whilst working, on average, a four day week. Similar schemes were introduced in Arizona (1981), Oregon (1982), Florida and Washington (1983).

Canada. In 1977, the Canadian government temporarily amended its UI Act to allow an experiment to evaluate short-time working compensation. Like California, this allowed UI benefits to be paid to workers for their workless days. Over a period of almost two years, 24 firms using short-time working were studied; on average hours were reduced in these firms by 20 per cent, for a period of 19 weeks. As Reid (1982) comments, the attitudes of employers to the scheme was, in general, 'highly favourable' with most indicating that they would use the scheme again if conditions warranted it and if the option were available. Workers involved were also favourably disposed to the scheme; indeed, given that it provided more leisure and only a small drop in income, it is perhaps not surprising that it was not only those directly threatened with redundancy who valued the scheme but also those not immediately faced with complete lay-off.

Since short-time working involves North American employers in continued payments of certain fringe benefits which would cease if workers were laid off (e.g. health insurance payments), short-time working involves a small increase in relative labour costs. Meltz *et al.* (1981, p. 24) have estimated this cost at between $\frac{1}{2}$ and 1 per cent of total labour costs. However, both Reid and Meltz *et al.* argue that this may be more than offset by avoiding the 'replacement costs' — rehiring, training, etc. — incurred if layoffs are used in preference to short-time working.

The Canadian experiment was terminated in 1979, but in 1982 a national scheme was introduced, which was used by 200,000 workers during that year. This represented a much higher response than had been anticipated; initially the budget for the short-time subsidy had been set at just $10 million but this was subsequently increased to $190 million (Montgomery, 1982). The terms of the scheme stated that worktime must be reduced by 10–60 per cent for a period of 6–26 weeks. In 1982 average actual work reduction of those benefiting from the scheme was 34 per cent (1.7 days), for a period of 21 weeks; average income maintenance was over four-fifths of previous earnings (Reid and Meltz, 1984).

Two of the most significant features to emerge from the North American evaluations of short-time working concern the characteristics of the groups working short-time, and trade union attitudes towards this practice.

Groups Most Affected by Short-time Working. Bednaznik (1980) has pointed out that among the average 1.6 million workers involved in (uncompensated) short-time working in the US in 1979, blacks, females, unskilled and semi-skilled manual workers were disproportionately represented. These groups also experienced longer periods of short-time working, along with older workers and those not unionized (Bednaznik, 1980, p. 7). Hence groups most subject to unemployment were also the ones most involved in short-time working. This suggests that the argument that short-time working creates a more equitable spread of the burden of insufficient work is, at best, only partially true. A study of the Californian short-time workers (Lammers and Lockwood, 1984) indicates a slightly wider spread of short-time working though these writers also argue that the short-time working provisions do not appear to protect disproportionately those groups most vulnerable to unemployment.

Trade Unions and Short-time Working. Just as trade unions in Britain have shown ambivalence to such working time changes as job sharing and reductions in overtime, North American unions have been equivocal over the value of short-time working schemes. Until recently in the United States, support for short-time working was no stronger than it had been 30 years previously. For example, whereas in the 1950s approximately 1 in 4 major collective bargaining agreements contained provision for reduced hours, this proportion had dropped to less than 1 in 5 by the mid-1970s (Bednaznik, 1980). Similarly, Slichter *et al.* noted as long ago as 1960 that 'the trend of union preference is more and more toward the restriction of work-sharing agreements'. Crucial to understanding this attitude is the primacy of the seniority principle in US unionism and the tendency for senior employees to prefer lay-offs rather than hours reductions, since under the former (on the principle of last hired, first fired) their own jobs are more likely to be unaffected (Best and Mattesich, 1980; Meltz *et al.* 1981; Rones, 1981). More favourable attitudes to short-time working among US unions were evident in the early 1980s, however, as the recession lengthened (MaCoy and Morand, 1984, p. 37).

In Canada, a significant divergence of union views on short-time working is evident between national and local levels. Whilst local union organizations have been influenced by immediate and short-run considerations and the favourable reactions of members to the compensated short-time working provision, at national level the Canadian Labor Congress has expressed far greater opposition to the scheme, on grounds such as its effect on diverting attention from the main problem of restoring full employment in Canada

(Reid, 1982). The enhanced take up of the scheme in 1982, however, may indicate that the continued high levels of unemployment reduced union opposition to arrangements designed to alleviate this situation, if only partially.

Evidence of union opposition to compensated short-time working has largely been absent in European countries. In Britain, support for short-time compensation has been expressed both at the level of the union federation (TUC, 1981, p. 44) and within individual unions, particularly those organizing industries badly hit by recession. Faced with large-scale redundancies it is not surprising that unions have ultimately supported schemes which encourage employers to adopt short-time working rather than redundancies, and guarantees for workers at least half of their normal earnings on the days they are without work. An additional factor influencing union attitudes is that even at the 50 per cent compensation level, most people remain financially better off compared to the social security entitlements they would otherwise receive for their workless days (TUC, 1981, p. 45).

Conclusions

In many European countries,[2] short-time compensation has become firmly established as a national manpower measure in response to economic downturn; similar systems are gradually taking hold in North America. Overall, reaction of both employers and employees appears positive. For employers, the system offers a flexible means of reacting to short periods of difficulty without disturbing the make-up of the workforce, or incurring costs either related to redundancy or any subsequent rehiring and training. For employees it not only helps to avoid (or at least postpone) redundancy but also involves only a moderate reduction in income. For unions the scheme offers the maintenance of membership levels, whilst for governments, such schemes appear to be not only less expensive than the alternative costs of redundant workers, but also politically preferable in maintaining a lower level of unemployment than would otherwise prevail.

Yet an important question remains: is short-time working compensation only useful in brief recessions, whilst faced with longer term downturns it acts to *postpone* rather than *avoid* redundancies? The length of time for which short-time compensation is paid is essentially an arbitrary decision; as we have seen this period ranges from 20 weeks in California and six months in Britain, up to a possible three years in certain industries in West Germany. It is these time periods and the length of the post-1979 recession which have made the evaluation of short-time working schemes problematic. In short, the central problem of temporary short-time working subsidies has turned out to be the *non-temporary* nature of the recent recession. Certain countries, such as West Germany, have responded to this by extending the maximum period of subsidy. In practice, however, a proportion of subsidies paid out at such time will go towards delaying rather than avoiding redundancies.

Given the stated benefits of short-time compensation, the length of eligibility for subsidy may be unduly short in many countries. Indeed if the eligibility period were extended — and in the case of Britain, if the regulation were also relaxed that jobs can only be 'saved' once through the subsidy — then it is feasible that this method of work-sharing could not only be part of a longer term strategy for overcoming an employment shortage, but also play a useful role in periods of slow recovery, when the increased pace of economic activity remains insufficient to bring about rapid and massive reductions in unemployment. This latter situation appears very likely in many countries in coming years.

Notes

1. Throughout this section, discussion is focused on short-time working *per se*, rather than lay-offs, which involves the complete suspension of a person's contract of employment for a period at the end of which the individual concerned has a recognized right to recommence his/her employment. For a discussion of lay-off procedures, see Grais (1983).

2. For a discussion of short-time working provision in Belgium, Denmark, France, Ireland, Italy, Luxembourg and the Netherlands, as well as countries discussed above (Canada, Germany, United Kingdom and United States), see Grais (1983).

6 PART-TIME WORKING AND JOB-SHARING

The widespread growth in part-time working has been a recent and rapid development. In the last 20 years, part-time work has represented a key feature of labour market dynamics and establsihed itself as a major element in the labour forces of industrialized countries. Despite this, the tendency to treat part-time workers as a secondary (and second class) labour force has continued, in part reflecting both the overwhelmingly female nature of part-time workforces and the way part-time work has been perceived by employers in the past. Yet the significance of part-time working in most contemporary industrial societies, coupled with its prospects for further growth in coming years, underline the need for a reappraisal of the role, value and rightful status of part-time employment. Additionally, in the longer term the distinction between 'part-time' and 'full-time' working is likely to become increasingly blurred (and as we shall see, the distinction is already often unclear and arbitrary) if total hours continue to decline and levels of individual discretion over working time expand. For this greater flexibility in working time to develop, however, the prejudices surrounding part-time work need to be recognized and challenged.

This chapter will first trace the growth of part-time working — its overall pattern, the extent to which it has been concentrated within certain sectors and groups of occupations, the reasons behind its growth (whether, for example, it is primarily demand or supply led). Further, following themes introduced earlier, the significance of part-time working in the overall pattern of working time will be considered, and in particular the extent to which it has contributed to a greater flexibility.

One of the aspects of part-time working which has attracted considerable attention in recent years is the concept of job-sharing, where two people jointly share the responsibilities of one full-time job. In the latter part of the chapter the arguments for and against job-sharing are examined, together with the developments which have already occurred in this area and the prospects for job-sharing in the future.

The Growth of Part-time Working in Britain

The increase in part-time working is one of the most marked changes in Britain's working time patterns in the past 20 years. Commenting on the overall development of employment in Britain between 1971 and 1981, Clark (1982) notes that the net increase of 360,000 employees in the working population in this period in fact represents an 800,000 decrease in the number of full-time workers and the creation of *more than one million part-time jobs*. By 1980 part-time workers accounted for over 20 per cent of the working population. As we shall see, whilst Britain has a higher part-time workforce than many other industrial countries, the trends evident in Britain are also occurring elsewhere.

As well as the size of the increase in part-time working during the 1970s — particularly significant in the light of the decline in full-time jobs — three particular aspects of that growth stand out. Firstly, the increase in part-time working was unevenly spread during that decade, with most of the growth occurring between 1971 and 1975. Between these years the proportion of the working population engaged in part-time employment rose from 15.5 to 19.1 per cent; in 1980, the proportion was 20.3 per cent (Clark, 1982). After 1979 the number of part-time jobs declined with the onset of recession, though the number in part-time jobs in 1981 was still considerably higher than the mid-70s total (Table 6.1).

Table 6.1 also illustrates the second major aspect of the pattern of part-time working during the 1970s: that it principally involved

Table 6.1: Trends in Part-time Working in Britain, Selected Years 1971–1981 (figures in thousands)

	1971	1972	1973	1974	1975	1976	1981	change % 1971–6	change % 1971–81
Total employees	21,648	21,650	22,182	22,297	22,313	22,048	21,314	1.8	−1.5
Male part-time nos.	584	600	665	689	697	699	718	19.7	22.9
Female part-time nos.	2,757	2,877	3,163	3,421	3,551	3,585	3,781	30.0	37.1

Sources: Annual Census of Employment, GB, *Employment Gazette*, August 1973, November 1977, December 1981.

a growth in *female* working. Most part-time work is carried out by women and most of the absolute increase in part-time jobs in the 1970s involved women. In fact, this growth in female part-time working accounts for much of the overall rise in the proportion of women in the total workforce, a proportion which rose from 38 to 42 per cent between 1971 and 1981 (Clark, 1982). Within the female labour force, the proportion working part-time in 1981 also stood at 42 per cent.

Most of the growth in female part-time working in the 1970s involved married rather than single women. In 1981 four-fifths of the female part-time workforce were married, compared to just over half (53 per cent) of the women working full-time (*Employment Gazette*, 1982).

Among the male part-time workers (5.9 per cent of all males in employment in 1981) many are located at the extremes of the working age range. Approximately one-third of male part-timers in 1981 were over the normal age of retirement, compared to less than 1 per cent of full-time workers. Additionally, one in seven part-time workers was under the age of 20 years, double the proportion of this age group in full-time employment (*Employment Gazette*, 1982).

The third main feature of the increase in part-time working in Britain in recent years has been its almost total concentration in the service sector. Overall, employment in the services grew substantially in the 1960s and 1970s, whilst employment in manufacturing and basic industries contracted. Between 1961 and 1981, total employment in Britain increased by 2.2 million, compared to a loss of 3.3 million jobs in mining, agriculture and manufacturing (Handy, 1984). In the years of fastest growth of part-time work (1971–76), 95 per cent of the part-time jobs created were in the service sector (Dex and Perry, 1984). By 1981, almost half (47 per cent) of all female jobs in the service sector were part-time. In the light of this trend for jobs to decline in manufacturing and increase in services, there is little to suggest that *direct* substitution of part-time for full-time jobs has occurred on a major scale so far in Britain (though because full-time workers have not maintained their overall share of employment, it could be argued that some indirect substitution has occurred). As discussed below, the substitution of part-time for formerly full-time jobs is a feature which may increase substantially in coming years.

A considerable proportion (40 per cent) of female part-time

Table 6.2: Industries with High Proportions of Part-time Female Working (000s), 1981

Industry	Female				Male	
	Part-time	Full-time	Total	% of female total working part-time	Total	(% part-time)
Retail Distribution	707.9	596	1303.9	54.3%	784.2	(17%)
Hotels and Catering	426.3	208.4	634.7	67.2%	318.3	(35.3%)
Cleaning Services	144.9	9.6	154.4	93.8%	37.7	(50.1%)

Source: Annual Census of Employment, *Employment Gazette*, 1981.

work is carried out in personal service occupations; in particular part-time working dominates total female employment in the retailing, hotel and catering and cleaning industries (Table 6.2). Hence a substantial proportion of part-time jobs are located in industries notorious for their low wages; another point we return to below.

Finally in this outline of the growth of part-time working in Britain, two further aspects are worth noting: the distribution of hours worked by part-time employees and the impact of the recent recession on part-time employment. In 1981, 43 per cent of part-time workers were employed for 16 hours per week or less — a vulnerable group since their hours fall below the threshold of obligation incorporated in much of Britain's recent employment protection legislation (covering among other things, maternity leave and redundancy payments). A further 35 per cent of part-timers were employed for between 17 and 24 hours weekly, the remainder working 25 to 30 hours.

Turning to the effects of recession, Figure 6.1 indicates that in terms of the employment sector as a whole, female part-time jobs declined slightly less rapidly than either full-time female or male jobs in the period of steepest decline in employment. Between March 1980 and December 1981, part-time female jobs fell by 4.9 per cent compared to a 6.5 per cent fall in full-time female jobs and 8.8 per cent reduction in male jobs. Additionally, part-time employment appears to have started to recover earlier and quicker than the other categories; between December 1981 and March 1983, female part-time employment increased by 4.9 per cent (to within

Figure 6.1: Changes in Employment, March 1980–March 1983, All Industries and Services

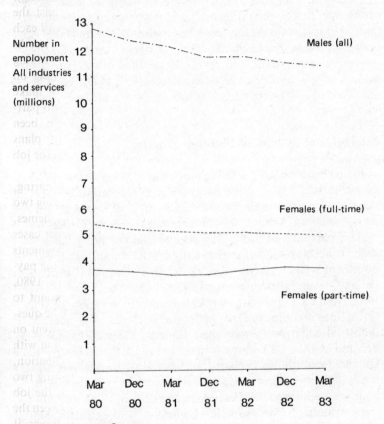

Source: *Employment Gazette.*

6,000 of its March 1980 level), whilst full-time female employment fell a further 2.7 per cent and male employment fell a further 2.9 per cent during that period.

In part, these figures reflect the smaller impact of the recession in the service sector, where female part-time working is concentrated. In manufacturing a different picture is evident with part-time working bearing a disproportionate amount of the reduction in female employment. Between March 1980 and December 1981, for example, the level of female part-time jobs in manufacturing fell by 19 per cent compared to a 15.7 per cent fall in the number of female full-time jobs. As far as manufacturing is concerned, therefore, this pattern is consistent with earlier business cycle fluctuations in the 1970s in which part-time working has been shown to decline more than its full-time counterpart in the downswing period (Dex and Perry, 1984). Again, consistent with earlier business cycle patterns, recent overall changes in employment continue to indicate part-time employment recovering quicker than other types; of the 263,000 new jobs created between March 1983 and March 1984, no less than 213,000 were part-time jobs for women (Lipsey, 1984).

International Patterns of Part-time Working

A major problem in comparing part-time working across different countries is the lack of a universally-accepted definition of what constitutes part-time employment. A number of broad definitions exist including that of the International Labour Office which defines part-time as 'work on a regular and voluntary basis for a daily or weekly period of substantially shorter duration than current normal or statutory hours of work' (ILO, 1973, p. 3). Clearly such definitions (and particular aspects within them such as what constitutes 'voluntary' part-time work) are open to a variety of operational interpretations. Data collecting agencies in a number of industrial countries (among them Canada, Finland, France, New Zealand and the UK) normally make the cut-off at 30 hours; in the US and Japan, however, part-time work is defined as less than 35 hours and one quarter of US part-time workers fall into the 30–34 hour per week range (see Deuterman and Brown, 1978). In addition, some countries (for example, Canada and the United States) normally include seasonal and casual part-time employees in their statistics (thus raising their reported level of part-time working substantially), whereas others record only permanent part-time employees. The US data also distinguishes between 'voluntary' and 'involuntary' part-time work, the latter resulting from a shortage of work at the workplace rather than through employee choice. Yet another basis for determining the level of part-time working (one adopted in the Labour Force Sample Surveys in the European Community) is to base judgement on whether the employees themselves consider their job to be full-time or part-time.[1]

The upshot of this definitional minestrone is a severe hampering in the drawing of fine distinctions in patterns across a large number

Table 6.3: Part-time Working in OECD Countries, 1981

	Males and females (% of total workforce)	Women's share in part-time employment (%)
	1981	1981
Australia	15.9	79.0
Belgium	6.4	86.2
Canada	13.5	72.0
Denmark	20.8	92.0
Finland	4.5	80.2
France	7.4	84.6
Germany	10.2	93.8
Greece	2.1	63.0
Ireland	3.1	68.6
Italy	2.7	64.1
Japan	10.0	67.3
Luxembourg	5.8	87.5
Netherlands	19.4	67.6
New Zealand	13.9	78.7
Norway	28.3	77.9
Sweden	25.2	84.5
UK	15.4	94.3
US	14.4	70.3

Source: OECD *Employment Outlook*, OECD, Paris, 1983, p. 44.

of countries. However, it is still possible to achieve at least some indication of the general level of part-time employment in different countries and the extent to which different trends, such as those identified in Britain, are also evident elsewhere. Table 6.3 indicates the extent of part-time working in OECD countries in 1981. The discrepancies in the figures for Britain (drawn by the OECD from EEC Labour Force Surveys) compared to the Department of Employment's own figures used in the preceding section, underline the disparities which arise from the different definitions of part-time work.

Table 6.3 indicates widespread differences in the amount of part-time working in different countries. Norway, for example, has a recorded proportion of part-time workers ten times that of Italy. The level of part-time working in Britain can be seen to be comparatively high, though significantly below that existing in Scandinavia. In the 1970s, the level of part-time working increased in most of the countries listed. In many cases this growth can be traced back much further; in the United States, for example, the number of part-time workers increased by almost 2½ times between 1954 and 1977 — a growth rate more than double the rate of increase in full-time workers (Deutermann and Brown, 1978). Similarly, in Australia, the number of part-timers more than doubled to 878,500 between 1964 and 1978, rising further to over one million by 1980 (Beasley, 1981).

Whilst this pattern of substantial growth appears to hold generally true for recent decades, the world recession after 1979 clearly exerted a substantial influence on the overall trend. The OECD has reported, however, that only in Britain did part-time employment actually decline between 1979 and 1981, though a number of other countries, including Australia, Belgium, France, New Zealand, North America and Scandinavia, experienced a significantly slower growth rate during this period (OECD, 1983).

Table 6.3 also indicates the high proportion of female workers in the total part-time workforce in different countries. The British case of women comprising four out of every five part-time workers was repeated in seven other countries in 1981; only two countries, Ireland and Italy — both countries with very low recorded levels of part-time employment — recorded a women's share in part-time employment lower than two-thirds. In addition, the British trend for much of the growth in female part-time working to be taken up by married women has also been evidenced abroad; in Australia, for example, married women comprised 52 per cent of all part-timers in 1964 but by 1978 this proportion had risen to 62 per cent (Beasley, 1981).

There are, however, certain exceptions to this general picture of part-time employment being dominated by married women. In North America, (and to a lesser extent in Australia), the number of young people engaged in part-time work appears much higher than elsewhere (though this is partly due to the way the US compiles its figures on part-time working, to include seasonal and casual part-time work). Between 1954 and 1977, persons under 25 years accounted for 45 per cent of the growth in voluntary part-time employment in the US (Deuterman and Brown, 1978). Similarly in Canada, young people figure prominently among part-time workers. In Ontario, for example, 44 per cent of part-time workers in 1976 were under 24 years, compared to 29 per cent between 25 and 44 years and 27 per cent aged 45 years and over (Meltz *et al.*, 1981). At the opposite end of the age range, the United States has also witnessed a growth in the proportion of older workers engaged in part-time work. Male workers over 65 years are also a significant feature of part-time working in France, Japan, Britain and the Federal Republic of Germany (OECD, 1983). Ireland and Italy also have a relatively high proportion of their part-time workers in the older age categories, though overall the level of part-time working in these countries remains low.

Finally in this section, just as in Britain part-time working is concentrated in the service sector, this pattern is also reflected elsewhere; in the EEC, for example, whilst only 5 per cent of persons in production industry worked part-time in 1981, this figure was almost 17 per cent in services.

Reasons for the Growth of Part-time Working

Several arguments have been put forward to explain the accelerated growth in part-time employment in the last two decades. These arguments fall into two broad categories, relating to changes in the demand for, and supply of, labour.

The Demand for Part-time Labour

The major change influencing the postwar pattern of demand for labour has been the growth of the service sector. As described above, the increase in part-time employment has been inextricably linked to the growth in services, with almost all the increase in part-time jobs located in service industries. In part, this reflects the character of manufacturing employment, especially the widespread decline in employment in manufacturing in recent years and the male-dominated nature of many manufacturing industries. In contrast the service sector has provided fertile ground for the growth of part-time working, owing to its high usage of female labour, the type of work involved and the non-standard hours which characterize many service activities (office cleaning, hotels, health services, restaurants, etc.).

A second factor increasing the demand for part-time workers is that on average they are cheaper to employ per hour than their full-time counterparts. In Britain, for example, average hourly pay of women part-time workers is around four-fifths that of full-time females; the level of average male part-time earnings is relatively lower at around two-thirds the full-time average (Glucklich and Snell, 1981). A similar picture is evident abroad; an OECD summary of the situation in nine industrial countries found only one

(Australia) where hourly earnings of part-time manual workers was not lower than those of full-time workers.

Such hourly earnings differences are due to several factors, including the concentration of part-timers in low paid jobs. Clearly a number of low paying industries do use a high proportion of part-time labour — hotels and office cleaning for example are not noted for their generosity when it comes to wages (Pearson, 1985). One study in the United States found that two-thirds of the difference in average hourly wages between part-timers and full-timers can be accounted for by the disproportionate number of part-timers in low paid industries (study cited by OECD, 1983, p. 51). However, the remaining one-third of the difference in the US study is suggestive of part-timers being used as cheap labour. This is supported by a survey in Britain which found that in 10 per cent of establishments, basic rates for part-time workers were less than their full-time equivalents in the same occupations (study cited by Equal Opportunities Commission, 1981, p. 3). One reason for this difference may be the rapid growth in the potential supply of part-time workers (for reasons discussed below) which has enabled vacancies to be filled despite the lower wages.

In addition to wage levels, there are other ways in which part-time workers may represent a lower cost to employers. In Britain, for example, employers (and employees) are exempt from paying National Insurance contributions for workers earning less than £35.50 per week (1985 level). Further, provisions of various protective legislation apply only to employees working at least 16 hours per week (or at least eight hours a week for those who have worked for the same employer for five years); the non-inclusion of those working fewer hours from this legislation means, in effect, that employers are not obliged to provide maternity payments, maternity leave, redundancy payments or meet possible costs arising from unfair dismissal claims. It has been estimated that one million part-timers in the UK are excluded from the main provisions of employment legislation (Leicester, 1982; see also Robinson and Wallace, 1984).

In addition, many part-time employees enjoy less favourable fringe benefits, such as sick pay, paid holidays and, in particular, pension schemes. On the latter, a survey of part-timers in Britain in 1977, indicated that in two-thirds of establishments where an occupational pension scheme existed, part-timers were excluded (Hurstfield, 1978). A later survey (1979) put the proportion of part-timers admitted to existing occupational pension schemes even lower, at 20 per cent (Equal Opportunities Commission, 1981).

Not all aspects of labour costs have worked in favour of increasing demand for part-time workers, however. There is considerable evidence, for example, of a widespread growth in non-wage labour costs (NWLCs) in most industrialized countries in recent years — recruitment costs, fringe benefits, social security payments, etc. (Hart, 1984). *A priori* these might be expected to stimulate the demand for more hours from existing employees rather than engaging more people to work relatively few hours, since the latter would make the 'fixed' proportion of labour costs (e.g. recruitment costs) relatively high. Indeed, in at least one country (Italy) the high social security contribution levied on employers of part-time workers appears to have been an important factor keeping the level of part-time working one of the lowest in Western industrialized countries (or at least the level of formal part-time working, since Italy maintains a thriving informal economy). In other countries, the effect on part-time employment of the increase in NWLCs appears to have been offset by the tendency for part-timers to be on lower salary grades and to enjoy less favourable fringe benefits; also, employers of the lowest paid part-timers in Britain are exempt from contributions to social security. Hence, the rise in NWLCs has in some aspects affected part-time employment to a lesser degree than full-time.

A third factor encouraging part-time work is the greater flexibility this offers employers, compared to full-time employees. A major development in retailing in recent years, for example, has been to increase manpower during periods of peak sales activity — between about 11 a.m. and 3 p.m. during weekdays and all day Saturday — by hiring part-time labour. For the employer, this enables manpower to be used selectively to cover peaks in demand, without incurring the costs of overcapacity during slacker periods. The growing awareness of the advantages of part-time work for efficient utilization of manpower is indicative of a more general change in attitudes towards part-time workers on the part of management. A survey conducted back in 1960, found employers' attitudes to be generally unfavourable towards part-time workers, who were regarded as less reliable and less loyal than their full-time counterparts and engaged mainly because of shortages of full-time workers and because, if necessary, they could be declared redundant more easily than full-timers (Klein, cited in Hurstfield, 1978).

Certain later surveys have shown a more positive attitude developing towards part-time work. A survey in Germany in 1977, for example, found companies taking a generally positive view of part-time work. Disadvantages such as additional equipment and administrative costs were seen to be outweighed by the part-time worker's contribution to profitability (measured in terms of greater efficiency per hour), a greater flexibility in the use of personnel, lower levels of accidents and absenteeism, and a smaller degree of fluctuation in output (Reyher *et al.*, 1980). Not all findings are consistently in this direction, however. In a study measuring perceptions of part-time workers towards their employment, Hurstfield (1978) found that half the respondents regarded their employers as holding unfavourable attitudes towards their part-time workers.

What of the future demand for part-time work? The pattern of new employment since March 1983 (see above) and the continuing shift in the emphasis of employment away from manufacturing and towards services both suggest the likelihood of a continued increase in the proportion of the total workforce employed part-time. Perhaps the biggest influence on future trends in part-time employment, however, will be the application of microelectronic technologies, particularly (in the short term, at least) in female-dominated occupations such as typing and clerical work. Clear evidence of this effect of new technology has not yet emerged, though there are signs in this direction from individual studies. In an investigation of banking in Canada, for example, Menzies (1981) reports new technology facilitating the increased use of part-time cashiers. This was seen to be partly due to the automation of transaction recording which previously had taken place after normal banking hours (pp. 47–8). The result was increased scope for bank cashiers to be part-time, employed only for those hours the bank opened to the public.

The Supply of Part-time Labour

The increase in part-time working reflects not only changes in industrial structure and demand for labour, but also how these changes have been echoed and reinforced by changes in the labour supply. The growing demand for part-time labour has been matched by a growing desire, particularly amongst married women, for employment. Where this desire has been felt by women still engaged in child-rearing activities, it has stimulated a demand for part-time employment which could be accommodated more easily with family responsibilities. Further, the variety of hours patterns which have been found to be subsumed under the title of 'part-time working' indicates the breadth of accommodation of employment with a wide range of domestic and other circumstances (Martin and Roberts, 1984).

Such has been the interest in employment among married women that at different times some growth in part-time working may be primarily attributed to these labour supply conditions — that is, during times of labour shortage (as in the 1960s), some employers were forced to fill posts with part-time workers due to their availability compared to the shortage of those seeking full-time employment. This appears to have been particularly true in a number of service industries such as retailing and catering which, for various reasons (including low average rates of pay) have been generally unattractive to men (Hurstfield, 1978).

Why should this desire among married women to gain employment have grown so substantially in the 1960s and 70s? Different commentators have pointed to a wide range of both objective and subjective factors, including the greater availability of part-time jobs, rising inflation, lower birth rates, increasing material aspirations, the greater social isolation of women (due to greater geographical mobility), growing male unemployment, a decline in the belief that 'a woman's place is in the home', and the growing lack of full-time opportunities (Mallier and Rosser, 1979; Clark, 1982; OECD, 1983). There is some indication that this last factor — the level of involuntary part-time working — has increased substantially in recent years; in Canada between 1975 and 1982 the level of involuntary part-timers rose from 11 to 25 per cent of the total part-time sector, and from 25 to 32 per cent in the United States (OECD, 1983).

Among other groups involved in part-time working, such as young people and older men, relevant factors explaining this supply of labour will include contributing to the cost of their education and using part-time work as a way of reducing work pressure (or responding to forced retirement) whilst at the same time maintaining both an interest and an income. The extension of this latter practice of 'phasing' retirement by interjecting a period of part-time work in between full-time employment and complete retirement, has received growing attention in recent years. Indeed in Sweden the practice has for some years received legislative support;

the Swedish scheme, and other aspects of phased retirement, are examined in Chapter 8.

Problems for Part-time Workers

Part-time working appears to contain a number of contrasting, if not contradictory, features, particularly in connection with people's attitudes to part-time working and the objective conditions of the majority of part-time work. On the one hand, there appears a strong potential demand among those not working and those in full-time employment, for a greater opportunity to work part-time. In their study of more than 3,000 female workers, for example, Martin and Roberts (1984) found that almost a third of the full-time workers said they would prefer a job with fewer hours per week. Other studies have shown a similar desire. In their study of more than 2,000 older workers, Makeham and Morgan (1980) found a large minority (44 per cent) in favour of moving to part-time working prior to full retirement (see Chapter 8 below). Added to this, levels of satisfaction among part-time workers seem generally high, both in relation to their hours of work and more generally with aspects of their job (Martin and Roberts, 1984; Leicester, 1982). Yet, on the other hand, most part-time jobs continue to suffer from lower wages, poorer promotion prospects and, for many — particularly those not covered by employment legislation — lower levels of job security, compared with their full-time counterparts.

How does this picture of relatively poor terms and conditions of employment tie in with the previous comments about high job satisfaction among the part-time workforce and the continued interest in part-time employment? Presumably (and it is necessary to rely on presumption and conjecture in the absence of empirical data specifically relating to this issue) the co-existence of contrasting objective and subjective conditions is partly explicable in terms of a lack of alternatives. Whilst social attitudes concerning domestic responsibilities remain substantially unaltered — that is, that women carry primary responsibility for child-rearing and various other household activities — then, for many, part-time work is not simply convenient but is the only practicable alternative to no paid employment at all. Given this situation, it is perhaps less surprising that so many part-timers indicate general satisfaction with their jobs, since the alternative appears to be a high level of 'cognitive dissonance' whereby a gap is created between expectations and the means to satisfy those expectations, which in turn leads to strain and frustration.

There are, however, some signs of a move to divorce part-time employment from its traditional characteristics of low status, poor pay and relative insecurity. One of the most publicized initiatives in this area in recent years has been the concept of 'job-sharing'. A brief review of some of the developments in this field indicates the possibilities for (and the obstacles to) using job-sharing as a means of improving the status of part-time work and increasing its potential for broadening the options in working time patterns.

The Growth of Job-sharing

The practice of job-sharing involves dividing one former full-time position between two part-time employees, whilst maintaining the status, promotion prospects, security and *pro rata* pay levels attached to the full-time post. Early demand for job-sharing schemes has come particularly from individuals and feminist movements seeking a pattern of working time less closely geared to the interests of males in single wage-earner households (Arkin and Dobrofsky, 1978). It has also been argued that besides working mothers, job-sharing would also find support among older workers — viewing it as a means of transition between full-time work and retirement — and workers of various ages wishing to combine employment with education (Olmstead, 1977). Job-sharing represents an attempt to develop a more flexible time framework for employment so that individuals and work organizations can create work arrangements which best suit individual and organizational needs and preferences.

Various specific claims have been made for job-sharing, both for the workers involved and their employers. For the former, because it entails the dividing of a full-time post, job-sharing potentially gives access to higher status, more fulfilling and better paid work than has typically been available to part-timers in the past, as well as in principle offering a more flexible work pattern that can be more satisfactorily integrated with outside responsibilities. For employers, job-sharing has been claimed to increase the potential degree of manpower flexibility, reduce absenteeism, maintain continuity in the event of one job-sharer leaving, help retain valued and experienced staff and more generally to allow 'an expanded range of skills and experience to be incorporated into a particular job title', whilst, at the same time, emphasizing 'cooperation rather than competition' (Olmstead, 1983, p. 482).

Various studies of small-scale and pilot schemes introduced in the USA, the UK and several European countries lend support to these arguments. In the largest of six reported studies of job-sharing, involving more than 100 job sharers in the Wisconsin civil service, McCarthy and Rosenberg (1981) found that labour turnover and absenteeism were lower among the job sharers, that productivity was higher and that costs of employing two job sharers were seen to be 'about the same' as employing one person full-time. Among the employees, there was also some indication that job satisfaction was higher among job-sharers than other co-workers. An earlier study of job-sharing couples in the United States (involving husbands and wives sharing the same or different jobs) also found this work arrangement to be viewed favourably, with the positive gains of increased leisure time, greater work flexibilities, and shared child-care and domestic responsibilities, outweighing any disadvantages (Arkin and Dobrofsky, 1978).

In Britain (as in other countries) job-sharing has made only very modest progress in terms of the total number of people involved, though as Figure 6.2 indicates, the range of occupations performed by job-sharers is considerable (at least in terms of non-manual occupations). Whilst some of these schemes are now relatively long-standing (e.g. job-sharing in the Lothian Health Board was introduced in 1975 as a means of retaining trained staff), one of the most highly publicized job-sharing schemes in Britain in recent years has been that operated by GEC in Coventry where some 88 school leavers began job-sharing in 1981, each working two and a half days. Stimulus for this scheme is said to have stemmed in part from reports of existing schemes working successfully elsewhere and also from the high level of youth unemployment in the West Midlands (Syrett, 1983). The prospect of unemployment, and more specifically the attempt to minimize lay-offs during an economic downturn, also prompted job-sharing schemes in two American airline companies in the early 1980s (United Airlines and Pan Am). Whilst the former used job-sharing among over 500 employees for two years and reportedly saved 365 jobs as a result, the latter introduced job-sharing initially for six months in 1980–1, and

Figure 6.2: Some Examples of Jobs Shared in Britain

Administrator	Probation Officer
Clerk/Typist	Production Worker
Doctor	Research Worker
Dry Cleaning Worker	Secretary
Journalist	Social Worker
Lawyer	Teacher
Librarian	TV Production Assistant

Source: *The Job-Sharing Project.*

reintroduced it in 1983 for over 170 flight attendants (Olmstead, 1983).

Hence various factors lie behind the introduction of job-sharing and whilst initial impetus in the USA appears to have emanated largely from employees, several factors have also led a number of employers to experiment with this form of work arrangement. Yet the fact remains that the practice of job-sharing (as distinct from the rhetoric surrounding the concept) is advancing only very slowly, with absolute numbers involved representing only a tiny fraction of the total engaged in part-time work. A brief review of some of the factors contributing to this lack of a significant 'take-off' of job-sharing illustrates some of the broader obstacles facing the more rapid introduction of greater worktime flexibility.

Some Reasons for the Slow Growth of Job-sharing

On the employer's side, two principal factors appear to be holding up a more rapid growth of job-sharing: inertia and an anticipated rise in labour costs. On the former, we have already seen how various aspects of working time (e.g. overtime) have not been subjected to the degree of management initiative which certain other elements of work organization have enjoyed (and suffered from) in recent years. Job-sharing is different to what has gone before, it does not fit automatically into established procedures for hiring, supervising, promoting or pensioning people. Further, whatever other claims are made for it, job-sharing is a form of part-time working, and whilst employer attitudes to part-time employment may be changing, preconceptions such as part-timers being less attached to their job than full-time counterparts, together with the perception of part-timers as a secondary rather than part of the primary workforce, are not easily dispelled. Additionally, if one of the employer's motives for introducing job-sharing is to retain existing staff (or fill vacancies), in times of wide-spread labour surplus (such as the 1980s) the need to offer unusual working time arrangements to maintain and/or attract labour is markedly reduced, if not removed. Hence, unlike working time developments such as early and phased retirement, which generally have the effect of reducing labour supply and manpower levels, the impetus to extend such options as job-sharing could be expected to be depressed during times of labour surplus, with interest rekindled in periods of manpower shortages (though this may not be the total picture, given the possible range of motives for introducing job-sharing. Used as a form of short-time working, for example, as in the American airlines cases, or introduced as a means of seeking greater efficiency, economic downturns could act to stimulate certain types of job-sharing, although in these instances the voluntary nature of job-sharing may be jeopardized).

Further, it is not only from among higher management that a reluctance to experiment with job-sharing (and other working time innovations) may emanate. Supervisors, too, may be unenthusiastic towards job-sharing, given the possible extra tasks which could be involved, particularly in the early stages (e.g. greater work co-ordination). The attitude of supervisors has indeed been identified as influential on the success of job-sharing schemes: 'The supervisor's role is critical in dividing work, scheduling, communication, resolving difficulties and evaluating the job-sharing team' (Diane Jones, an organizer of job-sharing in Wisconsin, quoted in McCarthy and Rosenberg, 1981, p. 134).

The Wisconsin experiment (see above) affected some 36 supervisors, who had mixed reactions to the scheme, and who cited such problems as additional interviewing requirements, need for additional workspace and lack of continuity in particular positions. Such were these problems that when asked if they would refill the position with two job sharers or one full-time worker, should the current sharers leave, almost half of the supervisors commented that they would revert to one full-time worker (McCarthy and Rosenberg, 1981).

As well as the apparent widespread lack of interest among management towards job-sharing, the negative, or at least indifferent, attitudes of most trade unions towards the subject exacerbates the inertia. In part, this may be seen to stem from a general lack of union enthusiasm towards part-time work which tends to be viewed suspiciously as a device employers adopt to undermine collective pay and other agreements. In addition, the negative attitude towards part-time working may also reflect the traditional male dominance of trade unions and the past difficulties which unions have experienced in recruiting part-timers. In the current period of labour surplus, union pressure has remained far more closely associated with seeking to protect and increase the number of full-time jobs than considering options for a greater level of part-time working among those who would prefer to do so. In his study of Australian unions, Benson (1982) found minimal interest in job-sharing; of the 20 unions in the survey, only three had developed policies towards job-sharing, and in each case this was one of opposition to the idea.

In recent years, however, some changes in trade union attitudes have become apparent, perhaps partly reflecting a growing awareness of the scale of part-time working, and possibly a belief among certain trade union leaders that the restoration of full employment through an increase in full-time jobs (as traditionally conceived) is increasingly unlikely without corresponding changes in working time arrangements (Jenkins and Sherman, 1979). In Britain, unions organizing local government employees, higher civil servants, journalists, electricians and probation officers have passed resolutions supporting job-sharing in recent years (Syrett, 1983, p. 44). A number of individual public sector unions in Britain, including NALGO and the National Association of Probation Officers, have negotiated job-sharing options at branch level in response to membership pressures for greater availability of part-time work (Equal Opportunities Commission, 1981). The EOC argues, however, that much greater union involvement is required to overcome employer reluctance towards job-sharing.

> The current experience of trade union involvement in job-sharing indicates that unions can play an important positive role in initiating and taking part in negotiations for an organisation-wide job-sharing policy; in assisting individuals negotiating from full-time work to job-sharing; and in ensuring the best possible terms and conditions for job-sharers. (Equal Opportunities Commission, 1981, p. 11).

On the question of costs, countries differ on whether it is more costly for employers to hire one full-time worker or two part-timers to do the same job. In Britain under the existing National Insurance arrangements (early 1985), the employer's contribution costs are identical for one full-timer or two sharers, up to the point at which the full-time wage is almost £14,000. Above this (the NI ceiling), the NI cost of the full-timer would remain constant whilst the contributions for the job sharers would continue to rise, until each was earning £14,000. The picture is different in other countries. As noted above, social security laws in Italy make part-time working expensive; likewise in France the comparatively low ceiling on earnings-related social security contributions can also make employers' costs for one full-timer much lower than for two part-timers (Manley and Sawbridge, 1980). In Canada it has been estimated that employers' contributions to statutory benefit plans would add approximately 2 per cent to the total labour costs for job sharers compared to full-time employees (Meltz *et al.*, 1981).

In addition, a number of extra costs may accrue to job-sharing, for example the administrative costs associated with processing two wages rather than one, two tax payments, two pension schemes, and two workers requiring greater supervision. Yet in most cases these costs are likely to be negligible; with many wage payments now computerized, for example, 'several more people on the payroll will make little or no difference to such a system' (Boyle, 1980, p. 51). One estimate suggested that these costs could amount to 'perhaps £20 per person a year' (Goodhart, 1982, p. 17). The question of greater supervision is likely to depend to a large extent on how effectively the sharers develop means of communication with one another, rather than relying on a supervisor for co-ordination. Other costs could include the additional expense of recruiting two people rather than one, and also extra workspace costs if the job being shared requires some degree of worktime overlap between the two sharers. The extra recruitment costs may be offset, however, if job-sharing is associated with a lower level of labour turnover, as has both been predicted and found (Equal Opportunities Commission, 1981, pp. 19–20; McCarthy and Rosenberg, 1981, p. 133).

Advocates of job-sharing argue that any short-term costs will usually be small and easily offset through the predicted higher productivity, reduced absenteeism, etc. Yet, at a time when pressure on employers to accommodate working time preferences both of existing staff and in the wider labour market, is low (due to the widespread labour surplus and general lack of job opportunities) any prospect of higher initial costs, coupled with possible organizational problems (e.g. relating to supervisory functions) are likely to increase the reluctance to experiment with new ideas in the field of part-time working. And whilst job-sharing appears to contain a number of advantages to offset any increase in costs, 'at the present time . . . those advantages do not seem to be widely recognized by employers since job-sharing has not been widely implemented' (Meltz *et al.*, 1981, p. 30).

Other obstacles which need to be overcome to stimulate a growth in job-sharing include current pension regulations and organizational rigidities. Older workers may suffer considerably from entering into job-sharing if this reduces their subsequent pension entitlement. In the Wisconsin study, for example, a prior survey had shown considerable interest in job-sharing among older workers. In the event, however, their actual participation in the job-sharing scheme was low due largely to concern over subsequent retirement benefits (McCarthy and Rosenberg, 1981). In Britain, occupational pensions are often calculated on the basis of earnings achieved in the three years prior to retirement; hence some protection of entitlement would be necessary for job-sharing to gain ground among older workers covered by company pension schemes. Another constraint on the development of job-sharing is the lack of experience in establishing career paths for job-sharers. 'At present, opportunities for promotion and transfer are relatively poor for job sharers' (Equal Opportunities Commission, 1981). Given the difficulties of assessing the relative promotional merits of two job-sharers compared to one full-time worker, this situation is likely to remain present for some time to come, at least until job-sharing is more fully accepted into the working time arrangements of work organizations.

With one or two exceptions, governments have done little to stimulate the growth of job-sharing, or the transfer from full-time to part-time work. In Britain as part of its job creation programme the Conservative government introduced a 'Job Splitting Scheme' (JSS) at the beginning of 1983, which offered a subsidy (£750) to those employers who split an existing full-time job into two part-time jobs, and as a result offered a part-time job to someone who was previously unemployed. Provision in the scheme's funding was made for at least 50,000 full-time jobs to be split. However, initial take-up of the scheme was very low; by April 1983 only 199 full-time jobs had been split (Incomes Data Services, 1983, p. 1).

Whilst clearly having certain similarities to job-sharing, organizations including trade unions and the Equal Opportunities Commission have been keen to point to important differences, which have led to a widespread condemnatory attitude towards job splitting.[2] In particular, whilst the basis of job-sharing is that the terms and conditions of the full-time post are protected, this is not necessarily the case under job splitting — those involved in a split may not necessarily gain the employment rights and security accruing to the full-time job. More generally, the ultimate objectives of job-sharing and job splitting are different. The former is primarily aimed at allowing employees to work a time pattern which facilitates the retention of an interesting job whilst also meeting outside responsibilities; the latter is aimed at reducing the size of the unemployment register (and incidentally by requiring that unemployed recruits be in receipt of either unemployment or supplementary benefit, attracting the criticism of discrimination, since this denies many women access to the scheme). Overall the picture is one of governments doing very little to stimulate job-sharing. If in coming years work-sharing arguments gain greater acceptance, then the obvious employment creating potential of job-sharing, coupled with the claims which have been made on its behalf, may result in a more favourable climate being created (e.g. via protection of pension entitlement, subsidies to overcome any transition costs, favourable amendments to laws governing social security contributions) to encourage this form of working time arrangement. Such a change in attitude towards job-sharing, however, does not yet appear to be on any immediate horizon.

Conclusions

In the last two decades, the growth in part-time working has represented a major modification to working time practices in both Britain and many other industrialized countries. The signs are that this growth is set to continue though not perhaps at its recent pace. With developments such as the continuing importance of the service sector and the further application of new technology, the time is probably not far off when one quarter of the British workforce is employed part-time. The previous strong growth in part-time working is attributable to the coincidence of demand and supply factors, with increased employer interest in expanding part-time working receiving a favourable response, particularly from married women seeking to obtain employment whilst at the same time continuing to fulfil a range of domestic responsibilities. This mutual reinforcement of labour demand and supply forces is likely to continue in the future, with on the one hand, employers seeking to optimize the labour input at times of heaviest workload, and on the other hand a desire to maintain and improve living conditions, counter the financial hardship of high unemployment, and seek fulfilment outside the home, acting to maintain a high level of (still predominantly female) part-time labour supply.

How much of this growth will take the form of job-sharing is more doubtful. Up to now the interest in job-sharing has been expressed more in words than deeds, and the institutional, organizational and attitudinal barriers facing a major growth in job-sharing are unlikely to be easily breached. On the positive side, reports on job-sharing schemes in operation offer employers encouraging signs on absenteeism, productivity, work scheduling, costs, etc. In addition, the central theme in the job-sharing argument — that this work arrangement is a means to both a rewarding job and meeting outside responsibilities — performs the important function of further underlining the inferior terms, conditions and nature of the work of many, if not most, part-time jobs. Only when the long-standing view of part-time work as inferior is dispelled (and the discriminatory rewards and conditions accruing to part-time work abolished), will part-time work and its job-sharing variant be more fully performing its valuable role of extending working time flexibility and discretion.

One development which could act to reduce the discrimination against part-timers is the undermining of the part-time/full-time distinction, following further reductions in full-time hours towards the 35 or 30 hour levels (the most typical definitional limits of what constitutes part-time work). Yet to achieve equality of treatment requires overcoming not simply a prejudice towards those whose working hours are shorter than others, but also tackling the persistent and much wider problem of sex discrimination. For just as the female section of the workforce continue to suffer widespread overt and covert discrimination (despite recent legislation; see Chiplin and Sloane, 1982), so too it is apparent that a central factor explaining why part-timers have not received fairer treatment in their terms and conditions of employment, etc., has been the overwhelmingly female nature of the part-time workforce.

Notes

1. Those wishing to delve further into the murky waters of how part-time work is defined could usefully begin with the Technical Annex of the OECD's *Employment Outlook*, September 1983.

2. The trade unions in Britain have been particularly critical of this scheme; at the time of its announcement in July 1982, the TUC leadership denounced it as 'a shoddy, cosmetic exercise' designed solely to mask the true extent of unemployment.

7 FLEXITIME, COMPRESSED WORKWEEKS AND STAGGERED HOURS

Some of the developments considered in previous chapters (such as the greater availability of compensated short-time working and part-time employment) have indirectly led to a greater flexibility, or at least a greater breadth in the overall pattern of working time. There have also been more direct attempts to increase flexibility of worktime, however, with the introduction of 'flexitime' arrangements in the 1970s. The development of flexitime, the extent to which it genuinely increases flexibility and the implications for broader increases in worktime discretion provides the focus of the first part of this chapter. Two other changes in worktime patterns are also considered: compressed workweeks and staggered hours; more attention is given to the former, however, due to its wider implications and the possibility that compressed weeks will become increasingly common as total working hours decline.

Flexitime

The practice of flexible working hours, or 'flexitime', came to the fore in the early 1970s. In different countries, various versions of flexitime exist, going under different titles such as 'flexitour', Gleitzeit ('gliding time'), maxiflex and variable day. The most common form of flexitime, however, is based on 'an arrangement whereby, within set limits, employees may vary their starting and finishing times to suit their own needs, provided that they are all present during a mandatory "core" period' (McEwan Young, 1981, p. 26). Whilst some early versions afforded only a very restricted flexibility, (particularly in America, for reasons discussed below), most schemes in Europe, and latterly elsewhere, have followed the pattern of allowing employees to vary (within limits) their pattern of daily and weekly hours, provided an agreed number of hours are worked within a pre-set period. Typically, 'in order to comply with their work contract, employees are expected to "settle" their work account by the end of a settlement period (this may be a day, a week, a month) but are often allowed to "carry over'' (a so-called debit/credit limit) from one settlement period to the next' (ibid., p. 26).

A typical scheme, therefore, would be one where employees can arrive between, say, 8 and 10 a.m., and leave between 4 and 6 p.m. The hours between 10 and 4 may be designated 'core' time when no time off is allowed (other than for a fixed lunch time), or may be split into two core periods separated by a flexible lunch break (see Figure 7.1).

Figure 7.1: Examples of Flexitime Arrangements

8 a.m.	9	10	11	12	1	2	3	4	5	6 p.m.
Flexible start time		Core time		Fixed lunch period		Core time			Flexible finish time	
Flexible start time		Core time		Flexible lunch period		Core time			Flexible finish time	

Much has been written on the advantages of flexitime, for both employers and employees. This literature deserves some attention, though as Lee (1981) and others have pointed out, much of it has been highly descriptive, uncritical and often eulogistic in tone, giving the impression that flexitime arrangements can be successfully applied in all situations. In recent years, a number of more thorough studies have been undertaken and these shed additional light on some (though not all) aspects of flexitime. To be able to evaluate its significance as a worktime arrangement, it is necessary to address four major questions:

(i) How widespread has been the development of flexitime and what indications are there for its future growth?

(ii) What have been the attitudes of employers and employees participating in flexitime arrangements?

(iii) What impact has this change in working time had on other aspects of employees' lives, such as family activities?

(iv) Given the 'clocking' procedures involved in formal systems, to what extent does flexitime bring about a net increase in employee discretion over worktime?

Patterns of Growth of Flextime

Formal systems of flexible working hours (in contrast to informal systems long established among professionals, senior non-manual grades and others) were first introduced in the Messerschmidt-Bolkow-Blolm aerospace company in West Germany in 1967, as a means of reducing congestion at starting and finishing times (Allenspach, 1975). Since 1970 flexitime has developed quite widely, though at markedly different rates in different countries. The general absence of national data on flexitime has led to considerable diversity in estimates of employees and companies affected. Nevertheless, it has been suggested that by 1971 some 2,000 companies in Europe had introduced flexitime for around one million workers (Wade, 1973, p. 19). Despite the shortcomings of available statistics it is clear that two countries — West Germany and Switzerland — have introduced flexitime far more extensively than elsewhere; estimates of 40–45 per cent of the workforces in these countries working flexitime have been reported (McEwan Young, 1981; 1982). In certain parts of Switzerland, such as Zurich and Winterthur, flexitime is said to cover up to 70 per cent of employees (Maric, 1977, p. 27).

Other countries which have introduced flexitime on a more modest scale include Scandinavia, Benelux, France, Italy, Spain, Canada, Japan, Australia, the USA and UK (Allenspach, 1975). In the US and UK, flexitime began to grow from 1971–2 onwards. In the United States, the first company to introduce flexitime was Control Data Corporation (in 1972) followed by several banks and insurance companies, and from 1974 onwards, in federal government (Bohen and Viveros-Long, 1981). Legislation in 1978 to amend the Fair Labor Standards Act encouraged greater flexibility in the US, by allowing more than eight hours a day to be worked without requiring overtime premia to be paid, provided that debit/credit hours were balanced each fortnight.

In the decade of the 1970s, flexitime appears to have grown at approximately the same pace in both the United States and the United Kingdom. A 1980 estimate for the UK suggested that around 8 per cent of the workforce (excluding professionals and managers) were involved in flexitime; the corresponding estimate for the US in the same year was 8.1 per cent, or 11.9 per cent if professionals, managers and salespeople were taken into account (McEwan Young, 1982; Nollen, 1982). The United States appears to have adopted flexitime more rapidly than its neighbour, Canada. A Canadian estimate published in 1980 indicated that around 150 companies and 30,000 employees were involved in flexitime, half of those working in insurance and provincial government (Fitzgibbon, 1980, p. 29).

Despite the significant growth of this work practice in several countries within a short period of time, the rate of adoption has generally not matched predictions made in the early and mid-seventies which suggested, for example, that up to 50 per cent of all workers in Britain could find themselves involved in flexitime (Sloane, 1975, p. 20; Maric, 1977, p. 32). Indications are that the spread of flexitime has slowed in recent years. This may be partly due to the general lack of innovation during recession, the widespread removal of recruitment shortages due to rising unemployment (one factor behind flexitime being to improve recruitment), and a reduced willingness by employers to incur the costs involved (e.g. the cost of time machinery). In addition, the *contingent* nature of flexitime may have become increasingly acknowledged (Legge, 1974), with employers recognizing that flexibility is more difficult to implement in some work situations than others (more on this below).

Furthermore, the trade unions in several countries have shown a generally sceptical attitude towards flexitime, partly because it has been seen as potentially open to abuse by employers seeking to exert pressure on employees to work long hours when the workload is heavy without receiving payment for overtime. At the same time it is arguable that the low priority given to flexitime issues by trade unions is another example of male bias within unions since a higher degree of flexibility could be particularly desirable for women trying to fulfil work and child-rearing responsibilities (Bohen and Viveros-Long, 1981, p. 64).

North American unions have frequently expressed criticism of flexitime, primarily on grounds that it threatens established criteria for paying overtime (Owen, 1979, pp. 105–6).[1] Likewise in France, unions have tended to be suspicious of flexitime, viewing it as potentially undermining existing privileges, as well as diverting attention away from other issues, such as pay and job security (Maric, 1977, p. 33). In contrast, in Germany trade unions in general, and works councils in particular, have been identified in a number of studies as performing a key role in flexitime's introduction (Wade, 1973; McEwan Young, 1982). A number of white-collar unions in Britain, including ASTMS, APEX and NALGO, have indicated a favourable attitude towards flexitime; further, a longitudinal study by Lee (1983b) suggests that between 1975 and

1981 trade union views (particularly in white-collar but also to some extent in blue-collar unions) showed signs of a more positive attitude towards flexitime in Britain, despite continued concerns such as that flexitime could distract attention from union campaigns for reduced hours.

Despite not fulfilling some early predictions of growth, the development of flexitime in the last decade and a half has nevertheless been quite impressive, particularly in comparison to the inertia which surrounds certain other aspects of working time. Yet flexitime has not developed equally within all industries and workgroups. Indeed, blue-collar workers generally, and those in small or medium-sized manufacturing establishments in particular, have gained little access to flexitime arrangements. In the United States flexitime activity has been concentrated in large-scale enterprises, mostly in the service sector and among non-manual workers. In Britain the picture is broadly similar though some blue-collar flexibility has developed, for example in the pharmaceutical industry (McEwan Young, 1982). In Germany and Switzerland, manual worker flexitime has developed to a greater extent, though still far less so than amongst their white-collar counterparts.

Assembly-line technology is viewed to be least compatible with the varying start and stop times inherent in flexitime, though even here examples of successful implementation do exist. In the Swiss watch industry, for example, flexibility has been created by allowing the build-up of up to three hours buffer stocks between work stations (Owen, 1977, p. 155). In addition to creating buffer stocks, those situations where advance production scheduling is possible, where employees work relatively independently of one another and where individuals have more than one skill and can undertake multiple tasks, have been identified as providing favourable production contexts for the introduction of flexitime (Nollen, 1982). The experience of flexitime growth in West Germany and Switzerland suggests that this worktime reorganization can indeed be extended to many blue-collar settings. Moreover, individual studies in Britain suggest that flexibility is also possible where a shift system operates (McEwan Young, 1978; see also Chapter 3). Overall, however, the lack of manual worker flexibility represents one more aspect of working time which differentiates white- and blue-collar workers, to the detriment of the latter.

On the future aspects for flexitime, it is possible that a renewed interest will accompany the increased application of new technology. 'New technology', argues Blandy (1984), 'should enable flexitime to be more easily organized and administered' (p. 441). At the moment the key word is *should* — there are as yet only a very small number of examples (other than the specific case of computers allowing more work to be done from home) of how increased flexibility in working time has resulted from new technology developments (for one such example, see Blandy, 1984, p. 442). However, three factors suggest that increased flexibility of worktime may accompany future new technology applications, partly as a means of securing employee co-operation and commitment to the changes:

— the potential of new technology for transforming traditional work practices, and thereby undermining existing bases of timing work;
— the creation of new demands on labour, including a need for greater utilization of expensive and rapidly obsolescent capital;
— the tendency for the implementation of new technology to be the subject of negotiation (or at least consultation) in workplaces where union representation is strong, due to the implications of changes for manning arrangements, skill requirements, supervision, productivity, etc.

Due to the root and branch changes to work methods which current technological developments are capable of bringing about, the progressive application of these technologies contains the potential for initiating a fresh agenda over how working time is organized. This is not simply a restatement of the adage about sharing out the fruits of productivity gains resulting from technological change. Rather it is an acknowledgement of the choices which become available for rearranging work, in the light of a fundamental change (of a progessive rather than an immediate sort) in the way goods and services are produced and manual and non-manual tasks fulfilled. Taken in conjunction with other changes occurring in industrialized economies — notably the growing importance of the service sector, the increasing feminization of the labour force and the continued short-fall in the total supply of jobs — the changes taking place create conditions suitable for an assessment of existing work patterns, an evaluation of alternatives and a pursuit of joint agreements to implement favourable worktime arrangements. We will return to this issue again in the concluding chapter.

Attitudes to Flexitime

As Robert Lee (1983a) has commented, 'Flexitime has had a good press, journalists and company personnel officers alike have praised its benefits for employees' (p. 297). Writers have also noted flexitime's potential links with lower absenteeism, fewer punctuality problems, easier recruitment, reductions in staff turnover, less overtime and higher productivity (Allenspach, 1975; Wade, 1973; Clutterbuck and Hill, 1981; Bohen and Viveros-Long, 1981; Nollen, 1982). A number of case studies have borne several of these relationships out, though the link between flexitime and productivity remains problematic, with certain studies identifying the presence of such a relationship (e.g. Pierce and Newstrom, 1983), whilst others have failed to do so (e.g. Orpin, 1981). Such discrepancies may offer further indication of the contingent nature of flexitime, and that it is more likely to have greater impact in some situations than others, depending on the existing work situation and the company's objectives in introducing the scheme (Lee and McEwan Young, 1977).

A number of advantages to employees working flexitime have also been identified, including 'greater freedom', improved 'adjustment to the individual's routine and life style', 'better use of leisure' and 'a better atmosphere at work' (Allenspach, 1975). Again, however, the studies are not unanimous on the extent to which flexitime influences employee attitudes, particularly concerning levels of job satisfaction. In the main, research has shown higher satisfaction under flexitime arrangements (e.g. Orpin, 1981; Wade, 1973) though there are notable exceptions which have failed to demonstrate any relationship between these two variables (Pierce and Newstrom, 1983). The latter authors highlight the mediating influence of employee perceptions of flexitime arrangements — only in those situations where a *significant degree of discretion* over worktime is seen to have been given to employees will job satisfaction be affected. That is, the flexitime system needs to offer sufficient flexibility for employees to value it. Other studies, (discussed below), also point to the negligible impact of restricted schemes.

The system that the flexitime is replacing is also likely to be important in influencing attitudes. As McEwan Young (1981, p. 26) has pointed out, employee attitudes are likely to be far more positive where flexitime replaces a time-clock controlled, rigid hours system, than where it is introduced to formalize and control a 'permissive' rigid hours system. Likewise, if flexitime is introduced partly in an attempt to reduce overtime payments (as some trade unions view it), the employee response is again likely to be mixed, if not hostile. Thus worker attitudes depend not only on the characteristics of the flexitime system itself, but also on management's objectives in introducing the scheme and the situation prevailing in the workplace prior to its introduction.

Two related sources of employee satisfaction with flexitime are likely to concern travel to work and time spent with family. On the former the evidence suggests that travelling time is indeed reduced by flexitime, by allowing journeys to be made outside peak rush hour. In a study of flexitime users in Seattle, for example, the proportion who commuted in the 7.30–8.30 a.m. rush hour dropped from 75 per cent before flexitime was introduced to 42 per cent afterwards (Martin, 1982). Another study reported by the same author indicated that employees on flexitime in Boston saved an average of two hours per week in commuting time, usually by selecting an earlier start time and travelling to work before the peak morning rush hour. Where there is a heavy reliance on public transport for travel to work, however, satisfaction with flexitime will be affected by the extent to which the transport systems offer adequate cover in off-peak periods. In a survey of flexitime users in a federal government department in Australia, for example, a quarter of the respondents indicated that lack of transport facilities constrained their ability to utilize flexitime (Plowman, 1977, p. 308).

Flexitime and Family Life

One of the major social arguments for flexitime is that it provides a greater degree of freedom to mesh together employment with other demands on time, in particular family responsibilities. Verifying this question has stimulated research both in Britain and North America. This work is part of a broader field of enquiry focusing on the impact of work on the family, and vice versa (Rapoport and Rapoport, 1978; Gutek *et al.*, 1981; Crouter, 1984). In the light of the claims made for flexitime, it is significant that one of the largest (American) studies of flexitime and family life found little impact of the former on the latter, when measured in terms of relative stress in the family, the amount of time spent in the family and the extent to which flexitime helped to equalize the sharing of family responsibilities (Bohen and Viveros-Long, 1981). A major factor in this study, however, was the limited nature of the flexitime under investigation. Employees (white-collar civil servants in this case) were restricted to choosing their time of arrival (between 7 and 9.30 a.m.), with little scope for day-to-day variation and with the requirement that eight hours had to be worked each day, with no debiting/crediting of hours from one day to another allowed (this study predated the changes in US legislation allowing variations from the eight hour day). Given these restrictions it is perhaps not surprising that relatively little influence on family life was found. As Nollen (1982) comments in his discussion of this study, 'Limited flexitime can have only limited effects' (p. 170).

Where flexitime offers a greater degree of discretion, a more significant impact on family life has been demonstrated. Both Winnett and Neale (1981) and Lee (1981) found flexitime increased the amount of time fathers spent with their children. Lee also found a reduction in the reported levels of stress related to child care. Yet, as in the Bohen and Viveros-Long study, Lee found little evidence of any equalizing of domestic tasks within the family, resulting from flexitime — in itself, the change in worktime arrangements was insufficient to effect a change in the (generally unequal) distribution of domestic responsibilities. Thus, consistent with several other studies of employee attitudes towards flexitime, a significant degree of flexibility can have a generally positive effect on family life, though in terms of its wider significance for the family, may exert a more modest influence than has at times been claimed.

Flexitime and Employee Discretion

As surviving organizations begin to recover from recession and new undertakings are established, one may anticipate renewed interest in flexitime arrangements, since established schemes have evidenced a number of advantages for employers and overall have been favourably received by employees. As Bohen and Viveros-Long (1981) note, the practice appears to provide a number of pay-offs at little expense;

Flexitime is agreeable because it costs very little and changes very little about what employers can expect by way of a day's work from employees — while apparently making people more cheerful about what they get paid to do (p. 199).

Yet there are several factors which could hold back the further development of flexitime. Included among these is a continued belief in its unsuitability in manual settings (despite some evidence to the contrary) and a management perception that flexitime not only undermines their prerogative (over the actual work pattern of subordinates) but also creates difficulties for communication and control where managers' and workers' schedules are different.

In the light of the finding that most flexitime arrangements in both Europe and the United States have stemmed from a management, rather than labour initiative (Bohen and Viveros-Long, 1981, p. 64), it would in fact be a little surprising if managers operating flexitime experienced a net loss in control. Indeed, in several respects management control may be seen to be *increased* by flexitime, any discretion gained by employees over start and stop times being offset by less discretion and greater accountability of time during the working day. For flexitime frequently involves a 'clocking' procedure, a practice in the past (and still so today) far more typically imposed upon blue-collar than white-collar workers, and one involving a degree of time accountability much greater than white-collar 'honour' systems.[2] For those subject to flexitime, the objective recording of hours (for example, via computer-linked clocking machinery) removes, or at least drastically reduces, management's task of monitoring punctuality; as a result, the time element of work discipline becomes to a greater extent self-supervised. Further, those occurrences where short absences have traditionally been allowed by many employers — for example, visits to the doctor — may tend to disappear under flexitime, further increasing the degree of managerial control over the number of hours worked. This potential of flexitime for increasing control over work time appears to be increasingly recognized by management. Lee (1980) argues, for example, that time recording equipment manufacturers have responded to management's view of flexitime as a control device both by marketing it more as a control system, and by offering additional infringement recording facilities.

Furthermore, whilst the benefits of greater flexibility are considerable, and the general concept very much in keeping with the arguments raised in the Introduction, at the same time it is important to recognize that in certain respects the flexibility afforded under such schemes is highly restricted. Individual schemes differ markedly in the flexibility they afford, for example the length of 'core' times, the period in which debit and credit hours must be balanced, and the degree to which hours may be carried over from one settlement period to the next.[3] Further, it is rare for the flexibility to be extended to the overall contract of employment, i.e. allowing employees to choose their total hours to be worked. There are a few exceptions, including a small number of German companies which have gone part way to developing a 'flexiyear' version of flexitime, by allowing individuals a degree of choice over the total number of hours they are contracted for annually (Teriet, 1977). On the whole, however, flexitime extends a degree of discretion over the beginning and ending of worktime, whilst the total number of hours remains fixed.

In other ways too the flexitime which has already been introduced is restricted in its scope and impact. Limitations in transport systems and rigidities in other institutional routines (e.g. school start and finish times) can reduce its value. More generally, given the continued inequalities in the domestic division of labour, the degree of flexibility generally offered represents an inadequate response to achieving integration of work and home life (though it is clear that any degree of flexitime is unlikely to achieve this, without an accompanying major shift in attitudes to gender roles). As we have seen, flexitime is limited too, in terms of the range of occupation and work settings it has been applied to and in the *net* increase in discretion it affords employees over their worktime.

Nevertheless, the experience of flexitime demonstrates that increasing choice over working time arrangements even by a relatively small amount can bring benefits to both management and worker and be accommodated in a variety of work settings. Studies conducted also suggest a positive relationship between the degree of flexibility afforded under the system and the level of satisfaction with it. From the employers' point of view, there is a point at which this relationship will break down, as added discretion begins to create problems for co-ordinating production, maintaining a service to the public, etc. There appears little indication, however, that this limit to discretion over worktime has been reached by present flexitime arrangements. On the contrary, the generally favourable way in which most schemes have been received may be seen as providing positive encouragement to exploring ways in which flexibility and choice over working time may be further extended.

Compressed Workweeks

One effect of many flexitime systems is to allow employees to compress some of their workweeks into fewer full working days. By building up credit hours through starting early and/or finishing late, employees can often take these hours in the form of a day or half-day away from work.

The arrangement of working contracted hours in fewer days has also developed independently of flexitime and in the early 1970s, workweek concepts such as '4 days, 40 hours' gained much publicity (Poor, 1972). Like flexitime, compressed workweeks are evident in a number of countries; the main developments, however, have taken place in North America and to a lesser extent in Australia. Yet as with flexitime, the early pace of growth of compressed weeks has not been sustained. The reasons for this slowing down, together with the factors encouraging the retention of compressed weeks by a significant number (albeit small proportion) of companies, provide further insight into the potential for varying working time patterns. Moreover, if one of the hindrances to a greater adoption of compressed weeks has been the overall hours required to be worked (and the time and physical pressures caused by concentrating those hours into fewer days), then a reduction in hours reopens the possibility for greater interest in compressed workweeks.

Forms and Growth of Compressed Workweeks

Weekly working hours have been compressed in a variety of ways, including 4 × 10 hour days, 3 × 12 hours and 4 × 9 hours plus a 4 hour half-day. Other alternatives have been intiated in particular countries, such as the '9 day fortnight' and the '19 day month' in Australia (Bell, 1974). In principle, the concept of compression does not involve a reduction in total hours, nor any extension in individual discretion over when the hours are worked; the central feature is the reallocation of worktime into fewer and longer blocks during the week. Some schemes, however, have been introduced not in isolation but in conjunction with a flexitime systems, thereby increasing to some extent the scope for employee choice (Harkness and Krupinski, 1977).

The assessment of whether a company's workweek schedule is compressed or not depends on the prevailing working hours norm. Early examples of compression include the British textile industry in the mid-nineteenth century, where the introduction of a shorter Saturday was accompanied by longer hours during the week which made up hours 'lost' on Saturday. This extended an older practice in textiles which involved the majority of the (few) holidays that were given also being made up by longer hours either beforehand or subsequently (Bienefeld, 1972, p. 39; see also Chapter 4).

More recently, as the five day week has become increasingly pervasive in Western industrialized societies, workweeks of 4½, 4 and 3 days represent the most common forms of compression.[4] Of these, the 4 day workweek has attracted most attention. Individual companies working a full-time four day schedule (that is, excluding those involved in temporary periods of short-time working) can be found in the United States as early as 1940 and in Australia in 1947 (Poor, 1972; Symons, 1978). The main growth period, however, was in the early 1970s and occurred principally in the United States. The rapidity of this growth is evidenced by the fact that in mid-1971, approximately 600 firms in the US were offering permanent 4 or 4½ day schedules to around 25,000 workers, equivalent to less than 0.1 per cent of the full-time workforce (Sloane, 1975). By mid-1973 this proportion of the total workforce affected by compressed workweeks had increased to 1.7 per cent, rising further to over 2 per cent by 1975 (Table 7.1). After 1975 the proportion of US workers on compressed weeks plateaued for several years (Nollen, 1982, suggests that the increased usage between 1979 and 1980 may have been in part due to an energy shortage in 1979). Of the 1.7 million people on compressed workweeks in the US in 1980, two-thirds (1.2 million) were working four day weeks. The overall increase in usage after 1973 reflects an increasing popularity of the four day week; the number working three or four and a half days remained fairly constant (see Hedges, 1980).

Dickson (1975) argues that the USA exported the concept of the four day week at the same time as it imported the idea of flexitime. The popularizing of the 4 day-40 hour theme by Poor (1972) is seen by Dickson as an important part of this export process. In practice, however, no other countries have adopted the idea to the same extent as in the US and even there it remains at a small (though in terms of numbers of employees involved, significant) level.

Table 7.1: Proportion of US Workforce Working a Compressed Workweek, 1973–1980

Year	Number working a compressed workweek (000s)	Total full-time workforce (excluding farm workers) (000s)	Percent of total on compressed workweek
1973	990	58,923	1.7
1974	1,108	59,442	1.9
1975	1,247	57,787	2.2
1976	1,271	59,700	2.1
1977	1,399	61,891	2.3
1978	1,400	63,943	2.2
1979	1,493	67,712	2.2
1980	1,700	62,963 (est)	2.7

Source: 1973–9 figs: J. N. Hedges, 'The workweek in 1979: fewer but longer workdays', *Monthly Labor Review*, Vol. 103, No. 8, August 1980, p. 31. 1980 figs: S. D. Nollen, *New York Schedules in Practice*, Van Nostrand, New York, 1982, p. 8.

Nevertheless, in a number of countries, various industries have introduced some form of compression on a significant scale. In Australia, for example, the 9 day fortnight has developed in the oil industry, together with the 4½ day week in the clothing industry (Symons, 1978, pp. 6–7). Yet even in Australia, where the idea of compression has received considerable publicity, the overall proportion of companies involved remains very small. A survey of over twelve hundred establishments in 1976, for example, found compressed workweeks operating in considerably less than 1 per cent of companies (Symons, 1978, p. 5). In Europe, examples of four day workweeks can be found in many countries, including France, Germany and Britain, though again the proportion of total labour force involved is tiny. The British experience with the 'Three Day Week' during the energy shortages of 1972 and 1974 appears to have subsequently encouraged a number of firms to introduce a compressed schedule on a more permanent basis (Sloane, 1975). Among shiftworkers, particularly night workers, compressed workweeks (4 or 4½ nights) are not uncommon in certain industries, including engineering. In Britain, the recent reductions in hours since 1979 may be encouraging greater use of a small compression (the 4½ day week), with some firms tending to respond to the relatively small reductions in weekly hours by slightly longer work schedules during the week, in order to finish at lunchtime on

Friday (see, for example, White, 1982, p. 13). Until systematic data is collected in European countries, however, evaluation of the compressed workweek must rely mainly on American and to a lesser extent, Australian, evidence.

Advantages and Disadvantages of Compression for Management and Workforce

Why have managers introduced compressed workweeks? What are the anticipated benefits over a five day schedule? Owen (1979) among others has suggested that many managers have initiated the shorter workweek principally as a means of improving employee morale, particularly in those settings where the job is not particularly demanding, mentally or physically. The latter factor is important in allowing a longer period on the job without significantly increasing fatigue levels, which if affected would tend to lower productivity and increase the rate of accidents.

Most early articles on the four day workweek attributed various managerial pay-offs to the arrangement, including increased morale, lower levels of absenteeism, easier recruitment and less overtime. Several later studies are rightly critical of some of these early claims, however, based as many of them were on guesses, impressions and indirect methods of data collection. Yet a number of the early claims appear to stand up at least partially to more careful, longitudinal study. Nord and Costigan (1973), for example, found that in the pharmaceutical company they investigated, lower absenteeism was not just a short-term effect of the four day week but was still evident a year later. Likewise, Ivancevich (1974) found job satisfaction and supervisor-assessed performance to be significantly higher among a group of 4 day, 40 hour workers after 13 months, compared to a control group on a 5 day, 40 hour schedule.

The existence of other studies which fail to show, for example, any increase in performance (e.g. Calvasina and Boxx, 1975), or an unequivocal employee response to the 4 day schedule (see below), suggests the *contingent* nature of the compressed schedule. Like flexitime, the compressed workweek is clearly more suitable to some types of organizations than others and for some workgroups more than others, with the result that its impact on measures such as performance and job satisfaction will vary according to the degree of fit between the worktime schedule and the different organizational characteristics (including the characteristics of the employees). Thus in terms of the claims both for and against a compressed workweek, from a managerial point of view a careful analysis of the nature of the production process or service and the pattern of customer requirements, will be critical in determining the net benefit of compression. Problems of coverage, scheduling, fatigue and even a greater disinclination to work following a longer time away from work, may outweigh any advantages of compression for management.

Inadequate consideration of these issues may help to explain the apparently high rate of abandonment of compressed workweek schemes, a rate which one study put as high as 28 per cent in the USA (Nollen, 1982, p. 68). This underlines the point that there appears to be a widespread lack of analysis of technological and organizational demands on worktime and a more general reluctance to evaluate either long-established worktime practices or new worktime innovations; this tends to be compounded by an evident unwillingness to consider employee preferences over working time.

For employees, the availability of longer leisure periods, improved access to daytime education courses and reduction in the number of weekly journeys to work, represent potentially significant benefits of compressed week working. Several studies indicate a positive employee response to compressed weeks. A study by Poor and Steele (1972) found as many as 92 per cent of employees working a 4 day week were favourably disposed to the arrangement. Similarly, Nord and Costigan (1973) found most employees (+80 per cent) in their study viewed the 4 day scheme positively both six weeks and one year after its introduction. A study of three firms in Britain working a compressed schedule similarly found a high proportion of workers who thought it represented an improvement in their working conditions (Sloane, 1975, p. 24).

Other studies, however, have identified somewhat lower proportions in favour of the four day week pattern (see for example Mahoney *et al.*, 1975; also Fottler, 1977). Several individual characteristics likely to be associated with positive views towards compression have been identified; younger workers, for example, tend to be more positively disposed to the idea, as do those in relatively low level jobs and with low levels of job satisfaction (Balch, 1974; Goodale and Aagaard, 1975; Dunham and Hawk, 1977). Extra fatigue associated with longer hours could help to explain why older workers may be less favourably disposed to compression. Among workers with low job satisfaction, the compressed option may be seen to offer an opportunity to spend more usable periods of time away from an unsatisfying situation. Similarly, a compressed workweek may help to alleviate some of the social and physiological problems associated with night-shift working, by providing longer periods of time away from work. Following an earlier point, however, the extent to which compression finds favour among various groups is likely to depend, in part at least, on the extent to which individuals are engaged in physically or mentally demanding tasks. Other related factors such as the timing and duration of rest pauses and the environmental conditions of work are also likely to be important.

The employee benefits of a compressed schedule must also be set against other potential drawbacks, such as greater difficulty in fulfilling family responsibilities on the longer workdays. Here again, individual circumstances will bear significantly on whether workers (and particularly women workers) on compressed schedules find the different work pattern coincides more or less satisfactorily with family commitments (e.g. on the one hand, by providing more full days for domestic activities, or on the other hand by allowing insufficient time on work days for domestic tasks). At least one study (Nord and Costigan, 1973) found women reacting more positively to the compressed schedule than men; according to these authors this may have resulted from the women's 'free' day being more structured by (and more valuable to) their domestic role, compared to their male counterparts who valued their less structured free time less highly.

Among workers' representative organizations, compressed workweeks are seen to contain other possible drawbacks. North American unions, for example, have in the past shown a general aversion to schemes which run contrary to the norm of paying overtime rates after a daily eight hours have been worked. Not all union movements are critical of the compressed workweek, however. A survey in Australia, for example, found that more than half (56 per cent) of the unions questioned were in favour of compression, particularly the 9 day fortnight (Hogan and Milton, 1980, p. 10). Yet for the trade union movement as a whole, the concept of compressed weeks is a secondary issue compared with the major campaigns for a progressive reduction in aggregate working time. Moreover, as with the case of flexitime, the notion of compressed weeks represents something of a dilemma for trade unions; on the one hand such ideas are favoured by some groups (e.g. younger workers), yet on the other hand the compressed week concept cuts across more traditional union objectives relating to the length of the working day and eligibility for overtime payments.

The question of appropriate union attitudes towards compression is further complicated by the possible employment consequences of this form of worktime arrangement. For rather than containing any work-sharing potential, their is some indication that compressed workweeks may be associated with up to a *trebling* of dual job holding or 'moonlighting' (Nollen, 1982, p. 20). In this aspect it is also conceivable that the provision of longer leisure blocks would stimulate a further growth in the already burgeoning DIY field, thus heightening the possibility of reduced employment in certain trades such as house-painting, car mechanics, joinery and gardening.

Future Prospects for the Compressed Workweek

In coming years, there are several factors which suggest a potential increase in the use of compressed workweeks. First, a major obstacle to the application of compression has been the total number of weekly working hours. Pressing 40 work hours into four or less days not only engenders problems of fatigue but, as noted above, brings with it a number of potential difficulties in terms of fulfilling non-work responsibilities. Yet should the average number of weekly hours continue to fall towards 35 hours, this could significantly increase the flexibility and attractiveness to employees of some form of compression. On a 7 hour day, 35 hour week schedule, for example, the move from a ten to a nine day fortnight could involve working only an extra 47 minutes per day. Similarly, a four day, 35 hour schedule would entail a working day of eight and three-quarter hours — significantly less than the ten hour pattern involved in a four day, 40 hour arrangement. With a 45 minute lunch break, the $4 \times 8\frac{3}{4}$ hours could be organized so that work began at 8 a.m. or 8.30 and finished at 5.30 or 6 p.m. — not a dramatically different pattern from many existing schedules, and not markedly out of step with many non-work institutions (such as forms of evening entertainment).

Another current development in time patterns — the increase in shiftworking — may stimulate renewed managerial interest in the concept of compressed weeks. Partly this would reflect an extension of existing arrangements whereby some shift workers already work a compressed schedule. In addition, however, a compressed workweek could represent one means by which management secured the necessary take-up among employees willing to work shifts. One such case was reported recently where, in order to encourage technicians to work a double-day shift system, management offered three choices of compressed workweek — a four day week, four weeks on followed by one week off, or four long weekends out of six (Blandy, 1984). Other developments which may increase the possibilities for further introduction of compressed workweeks include a decline in the physical effort required in some manual jobs (due partly to the development of more automated technologies) and a continued increase in the average distance people live from their work (which in turn enhances the incentive to reduce the number of journeys to and from work).

At the same time, a number of counter pressures may be identified which could act to limit any renewed growth in compression. These include the increasing significance of the personal service sector which, due to the importance of contact with customers, may impose added constraints on compression due to the need to maintain coverage. Further, the growing proportion of women in the workforce may influence employee preferences away from a compressed schedule, given the potential problems facing women of reconciling longer workdays with domestic responsibilities. The rise in the female element in the total workforce could also restrict the availability of introducing highly compressed (e.g. 3 × 12 hours) workweeks. In Britain, for example, current legislation restricts the amount of daily work hours undertaken by women and young people to 10 hours (or 10½ hours including overtime) on any weekday.

Finally, whilst in some respects the compression of work hours gives further indication of the potential variability of worktime arrangements, most existing schemes have not extended the degree of employee choice over worktime patterns. For in most of the schemes reported in the literature there is no indication of employees being able to choose between compression or a standard week, or to opt for one form of compression rather than another. The example of the technicians, cited above, and the linking of compressed weeks with flexible working hours seem by far the exception rather than the rule. In the light of the foregoing argument, that compression will appeal to some age groups more than others, to some levels more than others and possibly to one sex more than the other, then clearly any imposed system of compression is likely to lead to a perceived *deterioration* in working conditions for some groups. Again, the starting point for devising a more satisfactory system of arranging working hours appears to be a twin analysis of, on the one hand, organizational constraints and requirements and on the other hand, employee preferences; such an approach is more likely to be innovative if recognition is also given to the potential for flexibility and discretion over worktime and the capability of work organizations successfully to adapt to different forms of worktime patterns.

Staggered Hours

As well as making work hours subject to more individual flexibility, or compressing them into fewer days, another arrangement which has made less impact is the notion of staggering work hours, whereby different groups of employees within a single firm, or employees in several firms within a locality, start and finish work at different times. Thus rather than a common schedule for everybody (e.g. 9 a.m.–5.30 p.m.) this would involve management introducing a series of start times between, say, 8 a.m. and 9 a.m. and a corresponding series of finish times. Thus compared to the two previous modifications to working time practices we have discussed, staggered hours represents the least departure from a rigid schedule and affords little, if any, discretion to employees to choose a different pattern of working time.

The main impetus for staggered hours stems from a desire to reduce congestion either within the factory (e.g. around the clocking machine, the wash-room or the car park entrance/exit), or outside (the level of traffic congestion/public transport usage in the locality, etc). Proposals for staggering hours were mooted as long ago as 1920 in Britain (Sloane, 1975) and practical experiments undertaken in France as early as 1955 (Maric, 1977). In the following 30 years, however, the application of staggered hours has been highly restricted, though one or two notable exceptions exist (Sloane, 1975; Nollen, 1982). In a number of countries including Britain, a form of *de facto* staggering exists due to manual workers frequently starting and finishing work earlier than their white-collar counterparts (e.g. 8. a.m.–4.30 p.m., compared to 9. a.m.–5 or 5.30 p.m.).

Overall, however, the lack of development reflects the influence of several factors including the eclipsing of the notion of staggered work hours by the development of flexitime, which introduces a degree of staggering (though in a form which is less managerially controlled than typically envisaged under staggered hours schemes). Other problems include the difficulty of achieving inter-firm co-operation for introducing staggered hours within a geographical area and the considerable degree of staggering required to overcome congestion in large cities (which in turn raises issues of employees being required to work 'unsocial' hours). For these and other reasons, interest in staggered work hours has remained low both among employers' and worker organizations.

Notes

1. In a earlier article Owen (1977) also identifies the means of implementing flexitime as important for union attitudes and in particular the importance of union involvement in the early stages of implementation.

2. In this respect (if not in any other) flexitime may be seen to be contributing to the harmonizing of white-collar and blue-collar conditions, particularly as there has been some reduction over the last 20 years in Britain at least, in the proportion of manual workers subject to clocking (Arthurs and Kinnie, 1984).

3. Indeed, some schemes offer no real flexibility at all for employees. The conflict in British Rail in 1981 over 'flexible rostering', for example, concerned employees working a minimum of 35 hours per week and a maximum of 45 hours (and an average of 39 hours) and was aimed at increasing manpower utilization, and contained no increase (many would argue it actually entailed a decrease) in worker discretion over working time.

4. It is worth noting, however, that a degree of diversity remains over what con-stitutes a 'normal' week in terms of the number of days worked. In the United States, for example, more than 14 per cent of full-time non-farm wage and salary workers had a workweek of more than five days in 1979 (Hedges, 1980).

8 CHANGES IN RETIREMENT PATTERNS

Time changes are occurring not only in relation to the working day, the working week and the working year but also in relation to the working lifetime. Over the past decade, retirement patterns have undergone significant alteration; the average age of retirement has decreased in many countries, and a number of initiatives extending the flexibility of retirement have been introduced. More generally, continued increases in life expectancy and in some countries the progressive ageing of the population, are heightening the cost of supporting a larger retired population, and together have made retirement a key issue in working time patterns.

For the individual, the retirement decision is a fundamental one and represents one of the prime transitions people make during their working lives. For many, an array of mixed feelings surround this transition, with psychological adjustment generally impaired by such factors as the status attached to employment in contemporary industrial society and the many social and economic changes which retirement entails. Kelly (1982), for example, characterizes retirement as involving for most people both gains and losses, whilst the process of retiring itself is characterized as one of *detachment* from a particular set of circumstances and *attachment* to a new set. This 'swings and roundabouts' picture of retirement incorporates contrasting experiences such as, on the one hand, increased leisure time, greater opportunities to follow non-work interests and the chance to leave a dissatisfying job; and on the other hand, a reduction in social contacts, an increased awareness of growing old, the loss of a clear purpose in society and frequently, a substantial drop in income.

There is also a widespread belief that retirement is associated with a decline in health, though evidence on this is far from conclusive. In a review of the studies on health and retirement, Minkler (1981) points both to contradictory findings and to the methodological problems of separating the specific effect of retirement from related factors, including the normal link between old age and mortality. Indeed, to go on working can be just as unhealthy, if not more so. A recent study of French managers, for example, found

147

heart and artery diseases to be significantly greater among non-retirees than their retired counterparts (Vallery-Masson *et al.*, 1981).

Whilst the health effects of retirement are inconclusive, there is broader agreement that retirement is a potentially stressful life event involving a move from a clearly defined status, to what in contemporary industrial society is widely regarded as a more marginal status. One of the main arguments put forward to facilitate a successful adjustment to retirement is to increase the degree of *choice* over the retirement decision, making more flexible both the *age* at which people can retire and varying the options over the *rate* of retirement (see for example ILO, 1978b, pp. 38–9). Before examining some of the initiatives which have increased the degree of choice over retirement, however, it is important first to consider the general patterns of retirement prevailing in different countries and how these have been changing in recent years.

The General Age of Retirement

Even excluding the recent growth in early retirement opportunities different countries display significant variation in retirement ages. Table 8.1 indicates the position in Europe; whilst several countries have similar retirement ages to Britain (65 years for men and 60 years for women), others vary from this pattern, notably Scandinavia, West Germany, Ireland, Netherlands and Spain, who maintain the same retirement ages for both sexes.

A number of the Scandinavian countries have also traditionally operated a higher retirement age; in Norway, for example, the retirement age was lowered from 70 to 67 years only in 1973, and in Sweden from 67 to 65 years in 1976. In Denmark the general age of retirement is 67 years for men and women, though as discussed below, provision for earlier retirement has increased substantially in recent years and by the late 1970s only about half of Danish workers were continuing to work until they reached 67 years (ETUI, 1979, p. 31). In contrast in a number of Eastern European countries (e.g. Bulgaria, Czechoslovakia, Hungary, USSR and Yugoslavia), normal retirement ages are on average some years lower than in Western Europe (60 years men, 55 years women) (ILO, 1978b, pp. 72–3).

Just as Table 8.1 indicates a degree of international variation,

Table 8.1: Statutory or General Retirement Ages in Europe

	Men	Women
Austria	65	60
Belgium	65	60
Denmark	67	67
Finland	65	65
France	65	60
Federal Republic of Germany	65	65
Greece	65	60
Ireland	65	65
Italy	60–65	55–65
Luxembourg	65	60
Netherlands	65	65
Norway	67	67
Spain	65	65
Sweden	65	65
Switzerland	65	62
United Kingdom	65	60

Source: Various, including European Trade Union Institute, *Reduction of Working Hours in Western Europe*, Part 1, Brussels, 1979, p. 30.

so too certain workgroups within individual countries enjoy retirement ages which deviate from the national norm. In Italy, for example, the retirement age in the private sector is 60 years for men and 55 years for women, whilst in the public sector the official retirement age is 65 years for both men and women (though some provision exists for long-serving public servants to retire earlier). Similarly in Britain, different groups enjoy retirement ages which are higher (in the case of doctors, judges and university teachers, for example) or lower (firemen, policemen and football referees) than the general age at which a state pension becomes payable.

Outside Europe, the two industrialized countries which exhibit significant differences to the general retirement pattern are Japan and the USA. In Japan, the general compulsory age of retirement for men and women is 55 years. Since entitlement to a state pension does not begin until 65 years, however, many 'retired' Japanese workers in practice continue working for their company, though often with a different status and at a lower salary. In fact this retirement/re-employment system cannot be viewed separately from other personnel practices in Japan, notably the widespread moral obligation to continue to employ regular employees, and the maintenance of a strong link between wage level and length of service.

What compulsory retirement in Japan in practice means, therefore, is that both these obligations end or are at least modified when the worker reaches 55 years of age. The effect on wages, for example, is indicated by the following statistics published in Japan in 1971: 59 per cent of the re-employed continued to do the same work, but 76 per cent experienced a drop in status and 52 per cent experienced a drop in salary (Yoshio, 1980). This writer goes on to note that, 'If we include those who do not suffer wage cuts but also do not receive the customary wage increase given annually to all employees, it is clear that the large majority of rehired retirees experience a drop in real income' (p. 112).

In the United States, the strength of groups pursuing the interests of older people (notably the Gray Panthers) has led in recent years to a considerable extension of the rights of older workers in relation to compulsory retirement. A 1978 amendment to the 1967 Age Discrimination in Employment Act means that workers up to the age of 70 years, in establishments employing 20 or more people, are protected from compulsory retirement on grounds of age alone. For federal government employees the provisions of the amendment go even further, such that there is no maximum age limit for compulsory retirement solely on grounds of age. However, though the Act covers all workers, in practice it has benefited mainly white-collar and managerial grades, who have been able to contemplate longer working in part due to their frequently more interesting and less physically demanding jobs, compared to blue-collar workers (Casey and Bruche, 1983).

Yet whilst a degree of variation and change in the general age of retirement has been evident, by far the greatest activity within this aspect of working time in recent years has been the proliferation of early retirement schemes, primarily as a response to the reduction in demand for labour and continued high levels of unemployment.

Growth in Early Retirement Schemes

The period after 1979 is not the first in which older workers have been encouraged to bow out of the labour market before they reach the normal age of eligibility for a state pension. Parker (1982) has argued, for example, that to a large degree retirement policies have historically been economically motivated, with encouragement of earlier retirement more evident during times of overcapacity, low

Widespread use of early retirement has also been made in the French coal and steel industries whilst in West Germany, vehicle companies such as Opel and Volkswagen have introduced schemes enabling workers to retire at 59 years; ESSO AG of Hamburg have gone further by introducing a scheme enabling workers with 10 years service to retire at 55 years (TUC, 1983b). Similar examples can be found in most other Western industrialized countries and whilst the main impetus has been to reduce manpower, in particular cases other factors may include a desire to reduce the proportion of older workers in an organization, or to free promotion bottlenecks — labour turnover being considerably lower among older workers than their younger counterparts (Doering *et al.*, 1983).

Any anticipated benefits of early retirement for companies, however, must be set against the financial and other costs incurred. Indeed, the expense of early retirement schemes — particularly those offering generous terms — has been a stimulus to the search for alternatives, including the development of phased or partial retirement programmes. Before looking at these, however, the early retirement programmes introduced by the state require consideration.

State Early Retirement Schemes

Whilst companies have been making increased use of early retirement to reduce manpower, governments in a growing number of countries have been looking to early retirement as a way to create job opportunities for the younger unemployed. These national schemes have taken various forms. In France and West Germany, for example, workers can retire early if they have paid sufficient social security contributions; in Germany, men insured for at least 35 years have for some years been able to retire at 63 years and women at 60,[1] whereas in France since April 1983 all workers with sufficient social security contributions are eligible for retirement at 60. Similar schemes operate in Greece and Luxembourg and also in Denmark where workers of 60 years and over (and who have paid at least 5 years contributions during the previous 10 years) are eligible for an 'early retirement wage' until the age of normal pension entitlement. The Danish scheme proved far more popular than first envisaged. When introduced in 1979, it was expected that the take up would be 15,000–17,000 in the first year (out of a total eligible group of 80,000) but in the event the application was almost 25,000 in the first month (Danish Ministry of Labour, 1980).

Whilst these state schemes have aimed implicitly to alleviate the problem of unemployment, a small number of other schemes are linked more *directly* to job replacement. The British and Belgian schemes, for example, both contain a 'replacement condition', whereby employers co-operating with the scheme are required to replace the retiree with someone who is unemployed. In Belgium, where men aged 60 years and over and women of at least 55 years may retire early on a state allowance, this scheme is conditional upon their jobs being taken by a young unemployed person under 30 years of age. In Britain, the Job Release Scheme also contains a replacement condition. From its introduction in 1977 until the early 1980s, eligibility for the JRS was gradually extended to cover men aged 62 years and over and women of 59 years (together with disabled men of 60 years and over). However, since March 1984 the eligibility has been reduced to 64 year old men (with the female and disabled eligibility remaining unchanged).

This replacement condition is one factor which has limited the applications for JRS, which in an early evaluation was estimated at about 10–12 per cent of those eligible (Department of Employment, 1980). The take-up still represents a substantial number of people — between January 1977 and February 1984 a total of just over 262,000 had taken advantage of the scheme. The aim of many employers in recent years to reduce (rather than replace) manpower, however, coupled with the financial inducements offered by companies to enhance early retirement provisions, has meant in many cases that both employees and employers have preferred to effect early retirement through occupational pension schemes, rather than via the JRS. As the government's own evaluation has shown, applicants for JRS tend to be mainly from semi-skilled and unskilled occupations, on relatively low incomes, working for companies in which they have no access to an occupational pension scheme (Department of Employment, 1980). Given also the current rates of allowance for the JRS (from April 1984, £60.65 for a married person and £48 for a single person) which is equivalent only to approximately 30–40 per cent of the average manual wage[2] (before tax), early retirement under the JRS is likely to seem unattractive to higher paid manual and white-collar workers, unwilling to take a substantial drop in income. Furthermore, the restricted age eligibility of the JRS (compared for example to national early retirement schemes operating on the Continent) has also limited involvement in the British scheme.

In addition to those retiring early direct from employment, another category for whom early retirement has become a reality are those older workers who are unemployed. Unemployment tends to be more severe among older workers, especially those looking for manual work. In Britain in January 1985, more than 52 per cent of workers over 55 years had been unemployed for more than one year, compared to 45 per cent in the 25–54 year age group and 28 per cent of those under 25 years. Many of these older unemployed are *de facto* retired, since their chances of finding employment are slim and many have in fact ceased to look for work. In several countries, workers over a certain age and unemployed for more than a year can take early retirement; in West Germany, for example, the age is 60 years for men and women, whilst in Belgium, men of 60 years and over and women over 55 years can change their unemployed status to that of being retired. In Britian unemployed men and women are ineligible for retirement under the JRS. The arrangements for older unemployed men did change in April 1983, however, such that most men aged 60 years and over were no longer required to sign at an unemployment office to secure national insurance credits. As a result this group is no longer counted in the monthly unemployment totals; effectively this has led to the removal of approximately 160,000 men from the unemployment register.

What does the future hold for early retirement? First, whilst selective early retirement schemes are likely to continue, there are few signs of any imminent iniatives towards a general lowering of retirement age, at least in Britain. Evaluations of a general reduction have usually focused on the financial costs involved and the lower cost-effectiveness, in terms of a reduction in unemployment, compared to selective schemes. A study in 1978 estimated that a retirement age of 60 years for men and women in Britain, coupled with a replacement rate of two-thirds, could potentially reduce unemployment by almost 600,000. The net cost of this, however (the cost of extra pensions, partly offset by the reduction in unemployment payments and the taxation paid by those who found work), was estimated at £1,000 million (1978 prices) (Department of Employment, 1978a). A recent report from the Social Services Committee *did* recommend a small reduction in the male retirement age in Britain to 63 years, together with a raising of the female retirement age to a similar level; however, this committee also recommended that these measures should not be introduced before the 1990s (Social Services Committee, 1982).

The continued high level of unemployment, however, is likely to maintain or even increase the level of *ad hoc* early retirement. Indeed, the opportunities for early retirement may come to be used partly as a bargaining counter-offer by employers and governments in response to growing trade union demands for a shorter working week. This has recently occurred in West Germany where in response to the demand by the main metalworkers union, IG Metall, for a 35 hour week, Gesamtmetall, the engineers employers' federation, proposed an early retirement age of 59 years as a means of reducing total working time. In addition, the continued (and given a prolonged economic upturn, the likely accelerated) diffusion of technological developments, could result in a high level of job losses in certain industries, and hence a continued requirement for different ways of reducing manpower, including via early retirement schemes.

Yet, from the older worker's point of view, a key factor is the extent to which the early retirement option is *voluntary*, rather than compulsory redundancy by another name. As one would expect, there is some indication that the retirement adjustment process, measured in terms of satisfaction with retirement, is more successful among those perceiving their retirement decision as voluntary compared with those for whom the decision was a *fait accompli* (McGoldrick and Cooper, 1982). However, whilst voluntary early retirement options, particularly if they are supported by adequate income maintenance, substantially increase the degree of flexibility over the retirement decision, the emphasis on *early* retirement indicates the limitations of this flexibility and the extent to which the flexibility is dependent upon economic considerations, in particular a desire to reduce manpower levels (in the case of individual companies) or the overall supply of labour (in the case of governments). The American decision to extend the provision for later retirement (see above) appears very much the exception in the current economic climate. Indeed, the equal extension of flexibility to both sides of the existing standard retirement age is unlikely to gain widespread support whilst a high level of unemployment continues to represent the major domestic problem in many countries. In the meantime, however, certain other developments are occurring; another way in which flexibility has recently begun to increase at both a national and local level is via the provision of gradual forms of retirement. As we shall see, one of the factors behind this development is the growing cost to the employer of early retirement.

Gradual Retirement Schemes

For the majority of older workers, retirement is an abrupt change, from full-time employment to no employment at all. For the employee, 'gradual', 'phased' or 'partial' retirement represents a possible means of reducing the shock of this role change allowing a more gradual separation from work and thereby potentially reducing problems of adjustment. By focusing on the period prior to retirement, such schemes further increase flexibility in the retirement decision by increasing the choice over the *rate* of retirement, rather than simply the age of retirement. In practice, however, there are certain conditions under which some phased retirement schemes may not necessarily aid the adjustment process. Phasing can take the form of reductions in working time (our main focus here) and/or reductions in job responsibilities; either arrangement could create, for example, feelings of role 'ambiguity' associated with being neither fully employed nor retired. We will return to this issue below, after an outline of the different schemes already in operation.

Phasing by Time

Up to now, the development of phased retirement schemes has been modest in most countries, though there is considerable evidence that such schemes would be well supported if introduced with adequate income maintenance. An attitude survey in 1978, for example, of almost 9,000 people of working age in the European Community, found a strong predisposition towards the idea of gradual change from full-time work to retirement, by reducing working hours in several stages (Table 8.3). A more recent survey of older workers in Britain also found a markedly stronger preference for some form of reduced working week (44 per cent of the sample) than either for retiring early (28 per cent) or continuing to work full-time until normal retirement age (24 per cent) (Makeham and Morgan, 1980). Support for phased retirement has also been expressed in Britain by the CBI (1981) and the TUC; the House of Commons Social Services Committee commended gradual early retirement schemes in its recent Report, though stopped short of

Table 8.3: For or Against a Period of Transition Between Work and Retirement

	For (%)	Against (%)	Don't know (%)
Belgium	70	17	13
Denmark	78	13	9
Fed. Rep. of Germany	66	17	17
France	76	17	7
Ireland	64	21	15
Italy	69	19	12
Luxembourg	53	22	25
Netherlands	80	12	8
UK	72	20	8
Community Average	71	18	11

Source: *The Attitude of the Working Population to Retirement*, Commission of the European Communities, Brussels, 1978.

recommending that the state should finance such a scheme on a national basis (Social Services Committee, 1982).

Yet despite this level of interest, gradual retirement schemes have developed only slowly in most countries. In Britain, a recent study listed 26 companies which have introduced certain time reductions for older workers (Casey and Bruche, 1983). In most of these the phasing is limited to the final 6 to 12 months of work, or to increasing holiday entitlement in the last few years. In addition to this, in October 1983 a restricted type of gradual retirement scheme was introduced in Britain in the form of a part-time version of the Job Release Scheme, whereby men and women within one year of retirement can apply to reduce their hours and receive an allowance, provided their employer makes up the unworked hours by employing someone part-time who was formerly unemployed. However, early signs are that take-up of this scheme will be limited. After the first four months of operation a mere 26 people in Britain were receiving the allowance. This probably reflects both the relatively low level of allowance,[3] the age eligibility restrictions (see discussion of JRS, above) and the limited appeal to employers due to the replacement condition.

Outside Britain, some time reductions prior to retirement are available in certain French and West German industries. In France, over a thousand of the solidarity contracts signed between February 1982 and October 1983 were concerned with partial retirement (Incomes Data Services, 1984a, p. 2). In West Germany, the growing cost of early retirement schemes has been on stimulus to the development of partial retirement. Siemens AG, for example, have introduced a phased retirement option, to help reduce the costs of their early retirement programme. Siemens employees with at least 20 years service can opt to work 20 hours a week and receive 75 per cent of former gross pay, for a maximum of four years before retirement. Elsewhere, in the Netherlands, 'senior persons clauses' (*seniorenregelingen*) have been written into many industry collective agreements, which allow for reductions in working time prior to retirement. In the Dutch printing industry, for example, the hours of 61 year olds are reduced by an equivalent of 30 days per year, rising to the equivalent of 75 days for those aged 64 years (Casey and Bruche, 1983). By far the biggest strides in reduced time for older workers, however, have taken place in Sweden; due to its scale and a number of unique aspects, this Swedish scheme warrants closer examination.

The Swedish Partial Pension Scheme

Under the terms of the Swedish Partial Pensions Act (which took effect in 1976), workers aged between 60 and 65 years and who meet certain eligibility requirements (having been in employment for at least 10 years since the age of 45, and at least five of the previous twelve months), can apply to reduce their hours — by at least five, though they must continue working for at least 17 hours per week — and receive a partial pension which compensates for 50 per cent[4] of the loss in earnings. Subsequent pension entitlement is not affected by the scheme. Since its introduction in 1976, participation has grown considerably and in 1981, 64,641 people (well over a quarter of those eligible) were receiving partial pensions (see Blyton, 1984, for more details).

The most common reduction in hours is 20 (three-quarters of applicants have a 40 hour week); however, as Figure 8.1 illustrates, a range of hours reductions are represented in the scheme, particularly among female participants. Employers in Sweden agreed to co-operate with, and indeed fund, the scheme, the cost amounting to 0.5 per cent of the total wage bill. The employers are not obliged by law to accept applications to reduce hours, but in practice only a small number of applications appear to have been refused; one study (Crona, 1980) found that only three out of a total of over 400 applications examined had been blocked by the employer (though of course this does not take account of those

Figure 8.1: Reductions in Working Time of Employee Partial Pensioners (December 1981)

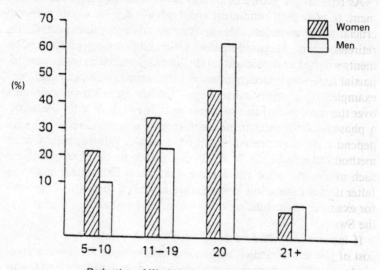

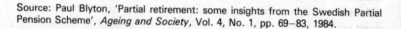

Reduction of Working Time (hours per week)

Source: Paul Blyton, 'Partial retirement: some insights from the Swedish Partial Pension Scheme', *Ageing and Society*, Vol. 4, No. 1, pp. 69–83, 1984.

potential applicants who were sufficiently discouraged by their employer's attitude that they never submitted an application for a partial pension). One of the most likely reasons why Swedish employers have been willing to co-operate with finance and accommodate the work adjustments entailed in the scheme, appears to be a desire to reduce their total volume of manpower, in response to the growing recession in the late 1970s and early 80s. Indeed, Crona found that partial pensions tended to be most common in private sector manufacturing companies who were already reducing manpower levels and/or who had a relatively high proportion of workers over 60 years.

Yet whilst the scheme may have a number of advantages for employers, it also appears to have been well received by older workers. In addition to the take up being higher than anticipated (which resulted in the financing having to be increased from ¼ to ½ per cent of the wage bill), a study of those participating in the scheme found that four-fifths of the sample thought that the partial pension would facilitate their transition from work to retirement (Crona, 1981).

As regards the future development of time-based phased retirement, the financial conditions attached to different schemes will be crucial to their success. Maintaining an adequate income prior to retirement and safeguarding both state and private pension entitlements will be key considerations influencing individual responses to partial retirement. Occupational pension entitlement in Britain, for example, is frequently calculated on the basis of earnings averaged over the three years prior to retirement. Thus significant take-up of a phased retirement scheme for a large number of people would depend to a large extent on modifications being made to this method of calculating occupational pension. Likewise, schemes such as the part-time Job Release Scheme in Britain are likely to falter if they offer a low level of compensation; the JRS allowance, for example, is considerably below that offered under the terms of the Swedish scheme.

If income levels are to be at least partially protected, then the cost of phased retirement to employers will also tend to be a factor hindering its development. Another obstacle may be a sustained economic upturn, which would act to ease pressures for manpower reductions and put increasing numbers of skilled occupations in short supply. There is some evidence that this is already happening. A recent case study of partial retirement in one West German company found management far more reluctant to grant the partial retirement (in the form of part-time working for two years preceding retirement) to craftsmen, foremen and machine operators, compared to unskilled workers (Kohli *et al.*, 1983). However, if the analysts are correct who argue that current and future generations of microelectronic technology will increase the options for part-time work, such a development could also act to support the further expansion of partial retirement schemes. Moreover, whilst the costs of partial retirement could be substantial (depending on the level and funding of income protection), such a scheme could turn out to be considerably less expensive than other early retirement options currently in operation.

Phasing by Job Changes

A long-established means of transition between working at full pace and retirement is for older workers to alter their work arrangements. This can take many forms, including termination of shiftworking, a change in method of payment or in job content — a job with fewer responsibilities perhaps, or requiring less physical strength. These changes may sometimes reflect the reduced health of an employee, or employers seeking to maintain high performance levels by substituting younger workers in place of their older colleagues, in certain areas of work. If involuntary, these schemes could potentially have considerable psychological impact on older workers, particularly if the job is of much lower status to the one formerly held. In the right circumstances, however — a voluntary choice or at least one reflecting the employee's reduced health — such schemes could represent a significant form of phased retirement by, for example, lessening the shock of a sudden reduction in responsibilities on retirement, or by contributing to an improvement in health prior to retiring.

In some countries, formal provisions have been agreed for older workers to amend their work arrangements. In France, for example, the provision for older workers to transfer from piece-rate pay systems to hourly wages is common and several industries allow older shift-workers the right to transfer to daytime working; exemption from overtime and shiftwork also exists in a number of Dutch industries (Casey and Bruche, 1983, pp. 7–13). In Britain, the practice of job transfer for older workers appears to be widespread, though no systematic information has been collected on this.

Conclusion

For many years a common theme in the retirement and general gerontology literature has concerned the likelihood that a continued rise in average life expectancy will tend progressively to increase the proportion of the population over the normal age of retirement. In fact in Britain this is not confirmed by current official estimates which suggest a picture of previous increases in the number of people over pension age levelling out at between 17 and 18 per cent of the total population (Fogarty, 1980). However, as Fogarty points out, this fairly stable picture could be altered by several factors, including a continued growth of early retirement, or a further increase in life expectancy (as a result of medical and social advances, for example, changes in cigarette smoking habits or the compulsory wearing of car seat-belts). The result could be a significant increase in the future proportion of the population reaching retirement age. One projection has indicated that with certain medical and social changes such as those mentioned above, the proportion in England and Wales of men of 65 + years and women aged 60 + years could reach 24.5 per cent by the year 2018 (Benjamin and Overton, 1980).

A growing proportion of older people in a society raises many different issues, from the costs of welfare provision and the overall patterns of demand for different goods and services, to the general political outlook which prevails. Two key issues for our discussion here are first, if more people are going to spend more time in retirement, then it is all the more important that their process of disengagement from work and attachment to retirement should be successful. Second, if health standards of older people continue to improve, this would seem to strengthen the case for greater flexibility over the age of retirement, particularly regarding access to employment after the normal age of retirement.

Clearly this flexibility is already available to a privileged minority — I write at a time when one of the two senior world leaders is over 70 years of age. However, in general, retirement patterns are only just starting to become less rigid and this has far more to do with the influence of economic factors on governments and employers than a general desire to increase the choices available to older workers. Moreover, the current economic climate has led largely to a growth in one directional flexibility, via an increase in *early* retirement opportunities. Any more balanced growth in flexibility, extending the opportunities for later as well as earlier retirement, will require one or more of a number of changes to occur. These include, for example, a more organized political lobby by older workers — a factor which appears to have played a significant role in increasing flexibility in American retirement practices; a greater recognition of the positive work attributes of older workers, such as higher internal motivation, less intention of leaving, and lower rates of voluntary absence and accidents, compared to their younger counterparts (Doering *et al.*, 1983); and/or a shift in the economic situation which leads to a shortage of manpower in general, and those skills held more or less exclusively by older workers, in particular.

Though true flexibility in retirement still seems a distant prospect, the changes which have occurred in the area of earlier retirement (and here, of course, we must be careful to distinguish between the voluntary early retirement schemes where choice is exercised, and the 'redundancy by another name' schemes, where choice is absent) represent a significant development in the overall pattern of working time. Furthermore, if the provision of partial retirement schemes was to expand, this could considerably increase the working time options for older workers, provided that sufficient attention was paid to the financial arrangements (level of income maintenance, protection of pension, etc.). The success of the Swedish scheme indicates the potential popularity of such a scheme, given suitable provisions.

Notes

1. Legislation passed in May 1984 in Germany allows some early retirement from 58 years. A pension is paid by the employer, but this is partially reimbursed by the state where an unemployed person is recruited as a replacement.

2. In April 1984, average manual earnings in Britain were approximately £154 per week, and averaged non-manual earnings £212 per week. Figures from *Employment Gazette*, February 1985.

3. In April 1984, the part-time allowance was £24 for a single person and £30.35 for a married person.

4. Reduced from 65 per cent in 1981.

9 THE FUTURE OF WORKING TIME

In the Introduction I argued the case for examining developments in working time across a range of aspects and drawing on the experience of several, rather than a single country. Clearly this approach has its dangers and its drawbacks, leaving some trends only thinly sketched, some issues only lighty covered, some of the broader wood obscured by the diversity of the trees under inspection. Despite the pitfalls in this approach, however, some elements of a more general pattern will hopefully have become apparent, though this pattern is itself comprised of strong elements of both continuity and change.

In terms of the quantitative aspects of working time, a gradual reduction has been evident, variously contributed to at different times by changes in weekly hours, holiday entitlement and the average age of retirement. Changes in the subjective, qualitative aspects of worktime, however, are more difficult to gauge. Some notable developments can be identified, including the growing availability of part-time as well as full-time schedules, a greater degree of choice for some over the timing of retirement, reductions in the relative importance of night-working and the introduction of flexitime systems in a significant proportion of work organizations. Yet it still remains the case that most people are subject to rigid worktime schedules offering little or no scope for exercising individual choice. What is more, not all aspects of working time have shown themselves to be receptive to change, reflecting in part deeply entrenched attitudes towards existing time structures and control over worktime. Moreover, not all changes to working time have improved the quality of the work experience — in those situations, for example, where reductions in time have been accompanied by an increase in the intensity of work.

Yet the examples of ways in which working time has become more diverse and open to a limited amount of individual discretion, together represent an important development, giving indication of the possibilities for greater choice over working time structures. In a period when traditional understandings of work and work organization are being challenged by circumstances both outside and inside the workplace — in particular the continuing shortage of employment and the fundamental changes in available technologies — this scope for working time flexibility and diversity assumes an added significance.

The future of working time is inextricably linked to the future of work. Work, or at least that part comprising paid employment, confronts two fundamental problems in this last decade and a half of the twentieth century: first, how to create *enough* jobs to satisfy the demand for work, and second, if sufficient jobs are created, how to ensure that their *quality* is sufficient to have made the effort of creating them worthwhile. The latter problem is many-faceted and clearly concerns existing jobs as well as those not yet created. Much has been written on what contributes to the quality of the work experience and widely differing views exist not only on the main factors influencing the subjective experience of work but also how these should be measured and evaluated.[1] There is a measure of agreement, however, on the importance to most working people of having at least *some influence over those decisions immediately affecting their own job.*

In both these problem areas — job creation and job quality — the nature of working time is of considerable importance. On job quality, from the individual worker's point of view, the ability to exercise greater choice over working time would represent a significant addition to his/her level of discretion in the workplace — extending worker influence beyond the way tasks are performed and the conditions under which they are performed, to the issue of for *how long* they are undertaken. Up to now, working time has been conspicuous by its absence in most discussions of industrial democracy and employee participation in decision-making.

In relation to job creation, the discussion has so far focused almost entirely on the concept of work-sharing. It is arguable that due to the way the work-sharing debate has been progressed, this has led to a too narrow examination of the issues and in the long run may even have been to some extent counter-productive in terms of the creation of a better organized pattern of working time. Partly this is due to the imprecise and generalized nature of the work-sharing debate. The notion of sharing work out more evenly has a beguiling simplicity, yet one which fails to reflect the complexities of actual worktime patterns and the relationship between working time and issues of cost and control. Moreover, much of the work-sharing discussion has assumed that all work contexts can be treated more or less equally for purposes of calculating the job-creating potential of different hours reductions, or the disposition of workgroups (all ages, income levels, etc.) towards work-sharing.

Together these factors have led to an oversimplified view of the link between time and jobs. Indeed, the whole notion of work-'sharing' has perhaps created a particular perspective characterized by negative connotations of underemployment and 'making the best of it'. There are still a number of important research tasks to be undertaken on work-sharing — identifying those situations (work groups or work tasks) which offer most potential for job creation, for example, together with the forms of time reduction most generative of extra employment and the significance of other factors mediating the relationship between hours and jobs. Yet the scale of the unemployment problem (both now and in the future) is such as to warrant a far more imaginative approach to working time. In particular the need appears to be for an approach starting with the dual questions of how much scope organizations can provide for a reorganization and rethinking of working time patterns and what room there is for workers to vary their work hours to match individual preferences. What the preceding chapters have illustrated is the change and diversity of working time, both between different work contexts and over time. There is nothing fixed or immutable about working time patterns — there is no unchallengeable organizational or indeed economic logic behind current patterns which prevents a re-evaluation of the suitability of existing patterns.

From the standpoint of the mid-1980s, and with the expectation that questions of the quantity and quality of jobs will remain prominent issues in coming years, two scenarios of working time developments may be imagined. The first (and most likely) is a continuation of trends already occurring, though with the pace of change varying between different organizations and industries, in different countries, and between different aspects of working time. By the end of the next decade most full-time workers would have reached a normal week approaching 35 hours (some a 32 hour week), with six weeks annual holiday and an average retirement age of between 58 and 60 years. With a working lifetime of approximately 40 years this would give an individual worktime total of approximately 65,000 hours — not so far removed from the 50,000 hours recommended by Handy (1984), though a long way above the

20,000 hours advocated by Gorz (1985), as a means of responding to the current and future shortage of paid employment. Yet while the reductions may be significant, this scenario is essentially conservative in approach, relying on the continued pursuit of current patterns and trends, whilst maintaining the rigidities and lack of choice of the present system (the inability to mix periods of education and employment, the continued distinction between full-time and part-time workers, restrictions over the retirement decision, etc).

This extrapolation of present activity would be unable to consider working time from a broader perspective due to its essentially incrementalist nature, typified both in legislative approaches to working time change and in agreements reached by collective bargaining. Neither of these mechanisms as they currently operate is geared to examining the problems of work and working time from a broader and longer term viewpoint. Yet individual, organizational and societal perspectives as well as a narrowly-defined economic perspective are fundamental to the question of what constitutes an optimum pattern of working time. At present these wider views gain a negligible, or at best only modest, hearing and exert little influence on current trends.

This broader approach would be the basis of the second scenario. Rather than the limited objective of pursuing a continuation of present trends, attention would be directed instead towards identifying the possible work patterns operable within an organization and matching these with the patterns of individual preference and societal need. It would be naive to expect a neat fit between these different perspectives, but at least this approach could stand as a basis for collective bargaining, thereby broadening that base from the narrow approach of seeking percentage changes to the *status quo* on hours, holidays, etc. This wider approach would require radical changes not only from management and unions (for example accepting responsibility to pursue work-sharing possibilities and creating conditions for greater individual discretion over worktime, rather than simply defining time boundaries) but also from government (e.g. removing financial disincentives to work sharing). Further, for management and unions this broader approach would require a less 'organicentric' approach to industrial relations, accepting the responsibility to examine working time (and other) issues in the light of community needs (notably, the need for greater employment) as well as in relation to the interests of those already within the workplace.

Clearly these two scenarios do not cover all the possibilities for working time developments. A stabilizing of working time patterns at their current levels could occur, for example, particularly if a return to relatively high rates of inflation took place, which in turn would give added priority to protecting income levels rather than increasing non-work time. Alternatively, working time trends of different groups could diverge, with much sought-after skill-holders being encouraged to work longer hours.[2] It is possible, however, that in practice working time will develop along lines which fall somewhere in between the two scenarios sketched above — that is, not simply an extrapolation of current trends, but nor a radical reappraisal of the objectives, limitations and optimum development of working time.

The relative position of the actual trend within the intermediate ground between the two scenarios will depend upon a number of factors. A long-term shift in work values, for example, away from the work ethic or consumerism would increase the perceived desirability of a work/income—leisure trade-off. At present there is little sign of such shifts in value patterns occurring on any significant scale, despite the growing experience of long-term unemployment and poor prospects for many entering the labour market. Yet if continuing technological developments bring with them the anticipated de-skilling consequences for many jobs, the resulting increase in boredom and lack of fulfilment could act to encourage such a shift in the value placed on work. Furthermore, technological change may have more direct impact on working time patterns, both by creating different organizational demands on worktime in order to optimize the technological potential, and also by providing the increases in productivity which could act as the basis for negotiating further working time decreases. It remains to be seen, however, whether the opportunities afforded by technological and other changes will be grasped to create a higher quality pattern of working time, containing the flexibility and choice to meet individual and societal needs and match more satisfactorily the different demands of work and non-work life.

Notes

1. This diversity is evidenced, for example, by the title of a book recently

published by Cook *et al.* (1981), *The Experience of Work: A Compendium and Review of 249 Measures and Their Use.*

2. Handy (1984) has recently noted the possibility of a rift developing between a small group of highly skilled technicians working, for example, 50 hours per week and a large group of low skilled and low paid workers employed for a much shorter period, such as 30 hours per week.

BIBLIOGRAPHY

Allen, R. (1980), *The Economic Effects of a Shorter Working Week*, Treasury Working Paper, No. 14, London.

Allenspach, H. (1975), *Flexible Working Hours*, International Labour Office, Geneva.

Arkin, W. and Dobrofsky, L. R. (1978), 'Job sharing', in Rapoport, R. and Rapoport, R. (eds), *Working Couples*, pp. 122–37, Routledge and Kegan Paul, London.

Arthurs, A. and Kinnie, N. (1984), 'Time up for clocking?', *Employee Relations*, Vol. 6, No. 3, pp. 22–5.

Balch, B. W. (1974), 'The four day week and the older workers', *Personnel Journal*, Vol. 53, No. 12, pp. 894–6.

Beasley, M. (1981), 'Permanent part-time work', in Wilkes, J. (ed.), *The Future of Work*, pp. 100–9, Allen and Unwin, Sydney.

Bednaznik, R. W. (1980), 'Work-sharing in the U.S.: its prevalence and duration', *Monthly Labor Review*, Vol. 103, No. 7, pp. 3–12.

Bell, R. L. (1974), 'New arrangements for the working week', *Personnel Practice Bulletin*, Vol. 30, No. 1, pp. 30–7.

Benjamin, B. and Overton E. (1980), *The Prospects for Mortality Decline in England and Wales*, Policy Studies Institute, London.

Benson, J. (1982), 'Trade union attitudes to job-sharing in Australia and some lessons for the UK', *Industrial Relations Journal*, Vol. 13, No. 3, pp. 13–19.

Best, F. (1980), *Flexible Life Scheduling: Breaking the Education-Work-Retirement Lockstep*, Praeger, New York.

―――― and Mattesich, J. (1980), 'Short-time compensation schemes in California and Europe', *Monthly Labor Review*, Vol. 103, No. 7, pp. 13–22.

Bienefeld, M. A. (1972), *Working Hours in British Industry: An Economic History*, Weidenfeld and Nicolson, London.

Blandy, A. (1984), 'New technology and flexible patterns of working time', *Employment Gazette*, Vol. 92, No. 10, pp. 439–44.

Blyton, P. (1982a), 'The industrial relations of work-sharing', *Industrial Relations Journal*, Vol. 13, No. 3, pp. 6–12.

―――― (1982b), 'Reorganizing working time', *International Social Science Journal*, Vol. 34, No. 1, pp. 149–56.

―――― (1984), 'Partial retirement: some insights from the Swedish Partial Pension Scheme', *Ageing and Society*, Vol. 4, No. 1, pp. 69–83.

―――― (1985), 'Workplace democracy, unemployment and the reduction of working time', *Economic and Industrial Democracy*, Vol. 6, No. 1, pp. 113–120.

―――― and Hill, S. (1981), 'The economics of worksharing', *National Westminster Bank Quarterly Review*, No. 136, pp. 37–45.

Bohen, H. H. and Viveros-Long, A. (1981), *Balancing Jobs and Family Life: Do Flexible Work Schedules Help?*, Temple University Press, Philadelphia.

Bolle, M., Fischer, U. and Strumpel, B. (1981), *Working Time in West Germany*, Anglo-German Foundation, London.

Bosworth, D. L. and Dawkins, P. J. (1978), 'Proposed changes in the extent and nature of shiftworking: some important policy issues', *Personnel Review*, Vol. 7, No. 4, pp. 32–5.

―――― and Dawkins, P. J. (1980), 'Shiftworking and unsocial hours, *Industrial*

Relations Journal, Vol. 11, No. 1, pp. 32–40.

——— and Dawkins, P. J. (1981), *Work Patterns: An Economic Analysis*, Gower, Aldershot.

——— Dawkins, P. J. and Westaway, A. J. (1981), 'Explaining the incidence of shiftworking in Great Britain', *Economic Journal*, Vol. 91, pp. 145–57.

Bourner, T. and Frost, P. (1985), 'The development of shiftworking', Dept. of Business Management Working Paper No. 7, Brighton Polytechnic, Sussex.

Boyle, A. (1980), *Job Sharing — A Study of the Costs, Benefits and Employment Rights of Job Sharers*, Equal Opportunities Commission, Manchester.

Bradlaugh, C. (1889), 'The eight hours movement', *New Review*, Vol. 1, pp. 124–39.

Brittan, S. (1983), 'Economic viewpoint', *Financial Times*, 6/10/83.

Brown, S. C. (1978), 'Moonlighting increased sharply in 1977, particularly among women', *Monthly Labor Review*, Vol. 101, No. 1, pp. 27–30.

Burgess, K. (1975), *The Origins of British Industrial Relations: The Nineteenth Century Experience*, Croom Helm, London.

Calvasina, E. J. and Boxx, W. R. (1975), 'Efficiency of workers on the four day workweek', *Academy of Management Journal*, Vol. 18, No. 3, pp. 604–10.

Carpentier, J. and Cazamian, P. (1977), *Nightwork*, International Labour Office, Geneva.

Casey, B. and Bruche, G. (1983), *Work or Retirement?*, Gower, Aldershot.

Cavendish, R. (1982), *Women on the Line*, Routledge and Kegan Paul, London.

CBI (Confederation of British Industry) (1980), *Jobs — Facing the Future*, CBI, London.

——— (1981), *The Will to Win*, CBI, London.

Chiplin, B. and Sloane, P. J. (1982), *Tackling Discrimination at the Workplace*, Cambridge University Press, Cambridge.

Clark, G. (1982), 'Recent developments in working patterns', *Employment Gazette*, Vol. 90, No. 7, pp. 284–8.

Clegg, H.A. (1976), *Trade Unionism Under Collective Bargaining*, Blackwell, Oxford.

Clutterbuck, D. and Hill, R. (1981), *The Re-Making of Work*, Grant McIntyre, London.

Cook, J. D., Hepworth, S. J., Wall, T. D. and Warr, P. B. (1981), *The Experience of Work: A Compendium and Review of 249 Measures and Their Use*, Academic Press, London.

Crona, G. (1980), 'Partial retirement in Sweden: development and experience', *Ageing and Work*, Vol. 2.

——— (1981), 'Partial retirement in Sweden', Paper presented at the 12th International Congress of Gerontology, Hamburg, 12–17 July.

Crouter, A. C. (1984), 'Spillover from family to work: the neglected side of the work-family interface', *Human Relations*, Vol. 37, No. 6, pp. 425–42.

Cuvillier, R. (1984), *The Reduction of Working Time*, International Labour Office, Geneva.

Danish Ministry of Labour (1980), *Labour Market and Labour Market Policies*, Ministry of Labour, Copenhagen.

Department of Employment (1978a), 'Measures to alleviate unemployment in the medium term: early retirement', *Department of Employment Gazette*, Vol. 86, No. 3, pp. 283–5.

——— (1978b), 'Measures to alleviate unemployment in the medium term: work-sharing', *Department of Employment Gazette*, Vol. 86, No. 4, pp. 400–2.

——— (1980), 'The job release scheme', *Employment Gazette*, Vol. 88, No. 7, pp. 720–6.

——— (1981), 'Pattern of holiday entitlement', *Employment Gazette*, Vol. 89, No. 12, pp. 534–5.

—— (1982), 'Trends in working hours', *Employment Gazette*, Vol. 90, No. 11, pp. 477–86.

—— (1984), 'Recent changes in hours and holiday entitlements', *Employment Gazette*, Vol. 92, No. 4, pp. 173–4.

Deuterman, W. V. and Brown, S. C. (1978), 'Voluntary part-time workers: a growing part of the labour force', *Monthly Labor Review*, Vol. 101, No. 6, pp. 3–10.

Dex, S. and Perry, S. M. (1984), 'Women's employment changes in the 1970s', *Employment Gazette*, Vol. 92, No. 4, pp. 151–64.

Dickson, P. (1975), *Work Revolution*, Allen and Unwin, London.

Doering, M., Rhodes, S. R. and Schuster, M. (1983), *The Aging Worker: Research and Recommendation*, Sage, Beverly Hills.

Dunham, R. B. and Hawk, D. L. (1977), 'The four day/forty hour week: who wants it?' *Academy of Management Journal*, Vol. 20, No. 4, p. 644–55.

Ehrenberg, R. G. and Schumann, P. L. (1982), *Longer Hours or More Jobs?*, Cornell, New York.

Equal Opportunities Commission (1981), *Job-Sharing: Improving the Quality and Availability of Part-Time Work*, EOC, Manchester.

European Industrial Relations Review (1985), *Report No. 132*, EIRR, London.

ETUI (European Trade Union Institute) (1979), *Reduction of Working Time in Western Europe, Part 1, The Present Situation*, ETUI, Brussels.

—— (1980), *The Reduction of Working Time in Western Europe, Part 2: Analysis of the Social and Economic Consequences*, ETUI, Brussels.

—— (1984a), *Collective Bargaining in Western Europe in 1983 and Prospects for 1984*, ETUI, Brussels.

—— (1984b), *Practical Experiences With The Reduction of Working Time in Western Europe*, ETUI, Brussels.

Evans, A. A. (1969), 'Work and Leisure, 1919–69', *International Labour Review*, Vol. 99, No. 1, pp. 35–59.

—— (1975), *Hours of Work in Industrialised Countries*, International Labour Office, Geneva.

Finn, P. (1981), 'The effects of shiftwork on the lives of employees', *Monthly Labor Review*, Vol. 104, No. 10, pp. 31–5.

Fitzgibbon, G. (1980), 'Flexible working hours: the Canadian experience', *Canadian Personnel and Industrial Relations Journal*, Vol. 27, No. 1, pp. 29–33.

Fogarty, M. P. (1980), *Retirement Age and Retirement Costs*, Report No. 592, Policy Studies Institute, London.

Fottler, M. D. (1977), 'Employee acceptance of a four day workweek', *Academy of Management Journal*, Vol. 20, No. 4, pp. 656–68.

Fudge, C. (1980), 'Night and day', *Employment Gazette*, Vol. 88, No. 10, pp. 1120–23.

Ginneken, W. van (1984), 'Employment and the reduction of the workweek: a comparison of seven European macro-economic models', *International Labour Review*, Vol. 123, No. 1, pp. 35–52.

Glucklich, P. and Snell, M. (1980), *Women, Work and Wages*, Low Pay Unit, London.

GMWU (General and Municipal Workers Union) (1979), 'A debate on shift-working', *Public Service*, November, pp. 10–11.

Goodale, J. G. and Aagaard, A. K. (1975), 'Factors relating to varying reactions to the four-day workweek', *Journal of Applied Psychology*, Vol. 60, No. 1, pp. 33–8.

Goodhart, P. (1982), *Stand on Your Own Four Feet: A Study of Work-Sharing and Job Splitting*, Bow Publications, London.

Gorz, A. (1985), *Paths to Paradise: On the Liberation From Work*, Pluto, London.

Grais, B. (1983), *Lay-Offs and Short-Time Working in Selected OECD Countries*, Organisation for Economic Cooperation and Development, Paris.

Gutek, B. A., Nakamura, C. Y. and Nieva, V. F. (1981), 'The interdependence of work and family roles', *Journal of Occupational Behaviour*, Vol. 2, No. 1, pp. 1–16.

Hadfield, R. A. and Gibbins, H. de B. (1892), *A Shorter Working Day*, Methuen, London.

Hallowell, A. I. (1937), 'Temporal orientation in western civilization and in a pre-literate society', *American Anthropology*, Vol. 39.

Hanami, T. (1980), *Labor Relations in Japan Today*, John Martin, London.

Handy, C. (1984), *The Future of Work*, Blackwell, Oxford.

Harkness, R. and Krupinski, B. (1977), 'Two surveys — working hours arrangements and shiftwork', *Work and People* (Journal of the Australian Dept. of Science and Technology), Vol. 3, No. 2, pp. 27–34.

Harriman, A. (1982), *The Work/Leisure Trade-Off: Reduced Work Time for Managers and Professionals*, Praeger, New York.

Harris, J. (1972), *Unemployment and Politics: A Study in English Social Policy*, Clarendon, Oxford.

Hart, R. A. (1984), *The Economics of Non-Wage Labour Costs*, Allen and Unwin, London.

Haulot, A. (1979), 'The staggering of annual holidays with pay', *International Labour Review*, Vol. 118, No. 2, pp. 191–204.

Hedges, J. N. (1980), 'The workweek in 1979: fewer but longer days', *Monthly Labor Review*, Vol. 103, No. 8, pp. 31–3.

—— and Taylor, D. E. (1980), 'Recent trends in worktime: hours edge downward', *Monthly Labor Review*, Vol. 103, No. 3, pp. 3–11.

Hill, S. (1983), 'The potential benefits of work sharing', *Financial Times*, 25/10/83, p. 17.

——, Blyton, P., Patrick, C. and Peregrine, J. (1984), *Decision-Making in the South Wales Engineering Industry*, Discussion Paper, UWIST, Cardiff.

Hogan, A. and Milton, P. (1980), 'Union and employer policies on alternative work patterns', *Work and People*, Vol. 6, No. 1, pp. 8–14.

Hughes, J. (1978a), 'The 35-hour week', in Barratt Brown, M., Coates, K., Fleet, K. and Hughes, J. (eds.), *Full Employment*, pp. 113–24, Spokesman, Nottingham.

—— (1978b), 'Three modest proposals', in Barratt Brown, M., Coates, K., Fleet, K. and Hughes, J., *Full Employment*, pp. 125–32, Spokesman, Nottingham.

Hunt, A. (1975), *Management Attitudes and Practices Towards Women at Work*, HMSO, London.

Hurstfield, J. (1978), *The Part-Time Trap*, Low Pay Unit, London.

Incomes Data Services (1983), *The Job Splitting Scheme*, IDS Study, No. 289, London.

—— (1984a), *International Report*, No. 208, IDS, London.

—— (1984b), *International Report*, No. 229, IDS, London.

Ingram, A. H. and Sloane, P. J. (1984), 'The growth of shiftwork in the British food, drink and tobacco industries', *Managerial and Decision Economics*, Vol. 5, No. 3, pp. 168–76.

Institute of Manpower Studies (1981), *Work-Sharing Potential — An Examination of Selected Firms*, IMS, Brighton, Sussex.

ILO (International Labour Office) (1973), *Part-Time Employment: An International Survey*, ILO, Geneva.

—— (1978a), *Management of Working Time in Industrialised Countries*, ILO, Geneva.

—— (1978b), *Older Workers: Work and Retirement*, ILO, Geneva.

—— (1984), *Working Time: Reduction of Hours of Work, Weekly Rest and Holidays with Pay*, ILO, Geneva.

Ivancevich, J. M. (1974), 'Effects of the shorter workweek on selected satisfaction and performance measures', *Journal of Applied Psychology*, Vol. 59, No. 6, pp. 717–21.

Jackson, M. (1984), 'Early retirement: recent trends and implications', *Industrial Relations Journal*, Vol. 15, No. 3, pp. 21–9.

Jenkins, C. and Sherman, B. (1979), *The Collapse of Work*, Eyre Methuen, London.

Jones, S. G. (1985), 'The worksharing debate in Western Europe', *National Westminster Bank Quarterly Review*, February, pp. 30–41.

Katz, R. and Goldberg, A. I. (1982), 'Working extra hours: worker involvement in the modern era', *Personnel Review*, Vol. 11, No. 1, pp. 31–4.

Kelly, G. (1982), 'Orientations towards retirement: a predictable transition', *Personnel Review*, Vol. 11, No. 3, pp. 33–7.

Kohli, M., Rosennow, J. and Wolf, J. (1983), 'The social construction of ageing through work: economic structure and life world', *Ageing and Society*, Vol. 3, pp. 23–42.

Kotaro, T. (1980), 'The effect of reductions in working hours on productivity', in Nishikawa, S. (ed.), *The labor market in Japan*, pp. 67–83, University of Tokyo Press, Tokyo.

Lammers, J. and Lockwood, T. (1984), 'The California experiment', in MaCoy, R. and Morand, M. (eds.), *short-time compensation: a formula for worksharing*, pp. 61–81, Pergamon Press, New York.

Landes, D. (1983), *Revolution in Time: Clocks and the Making of the Modern World*, Belknap, Harvard, Mass.

Lee, R. A. (1980), 'Recent trends in the managerial use of flexible working hours', *Personnel Review*, Vol. 9, No. 3, pp. 51–3.

—— (1981), 'The effects of flexitime on family life — some implications for managers', *Personnel Review*, Vol. 10, No. 3, pp. 31–5.

—— (1983a), 'Flexitime and conjugal roles', *Journal of Occupational Behaviour*, Vol. 4, pp. 297–315.

—— (1983b), 'Trade union attitudes to flexible working hours', *Industrial Relations Journal*, Vol. 14, No. 1, pp. 80–3.

—— and McEwan Young, W. (1977), 'A contingency approach to work week structuring', *Personnel Review*, Vol. 6, No. 2, pp. 45–56.

Legge, K. (1974), 'Flexible working hours — panacea or placebo?', *Management Decision*, Vol. 12, No. 5, pp. 264–80.

Lehmann, P. (1980), 'The National Institute for Occupational Safety and Health: expanding the frontiers of knowledge', in MacLaury, J. (ed.), *Protecting People at Work*, US Dept. of Labor, Washington.

Leicester, C. (1982), 'Towards a fully part-time Britain', *Personnel Management*, Vol. 14, No. 6, pp. 28–31.

Leontief, W. W. (1982), 'The distribution of work and income', *Scientific American*, Vol. 247, No. 3, pp. 152–64.

Levitan, S. A. and Belous, R. S. (1977), 'Work-sharing initiatives at home and abroad', *Monthly Labour Review*, Vol. 100, No. 9, pp. 16–20.

Lipsey, D. (1984), 'Jobs for the girls', *Sunday Times*, 22/7/84, p. 49.

Littler, C. R. (1982), *The Development of the Labour Process in Capitalist Societies*, Heinemann, London.

—— and Salaman, G. (1984), *Class at Work*, Batsford, London.

Long, P. (1981), *Retirement: Planned Liberation?*, Institute of Personnel Management, London.

Lydall, H. (1984), *Yugoslav Socialism: Theory and Practice*, Clarendon Press,

Oxford.

McCarthy, M. E. and Rosenberg, G. S. (1981), *Work Sharing: Case Studies*, Upjohn Institute for Employment Research, Kalamazoo, Michigan.

MaCoy, R. and Morand, M. (eds.) (1984), *Short-Time Compensations: A Formula for Work-Sharing*, Pergamon Press, New York.

McEwan Young, W. (1978), 'Flexible working arrangements in continuous shift production', *Personnel Review*. Vol. 7, No. 3, pp. 12–19.

—— (1981), 'Innovations in work patterns', *Personnel Review*, Vol. 10, No. 3, pp. 23–30.

—— (1982), 'Flexitime for production workers in Britain and Germany', in Nollen, S. D. (ed.), *New Work Schedules in Practice: Managing Time In A Changing Society*, pp. 33–53, Van Nostrand, New York.

McGoldrick, A. E. and Cooper, C. L. (1982), Minutes of Evidence, House of Commons Social Services Committee, *Age of Retirement*, HMSO, London.

Mahoney, T. A., Newman, J. M. and Frost, P. J. (1975), 'Workers' perceptions of the four day week', *California Management Review*, Vol. 18, pp. 31–5.

Makeham, P. and Morgan, P. (1980), *Evaluation of the Job Release Scheme*, Department of Employment, Research Paper No. 13, HMSO, London.

Mallier, A. T. and Rosser, M. J. (1979), 'The changing role of women in the British economy', *National Westminster Bank Quarterly Review*, pp. 54–65.

Manley, P. and Sawbridge, D. (1980), 'Women at work', *Lloyds Bank Review*, No. 135.

Mann, F. C. (1965), 'Shiftwork and the shorter workweek', in Dankert, C. E., Mann, F. C. and Northrup, H. R. (eds.), *Hours of Work*, Harper and Row, New York.

Mann, T. (1967), *Memoirs*, MacGibbon and Kee, London.

Maric, D. (1977), *Adapting Working Hours to Modern Needs*, International Labour Office, Geneva.

Martin, J. and Roberts, C. (1984), *Women and Employment: A Lifetime Perspective*, HMSO, London.

Martin, V. H. (1982), 'Energy savings and transportation efficiency from new work patterns', in Nollen, S. D. (ed.), *New Work Schedules in Practice: Managing Time in a Changing Society*, pp. 212–50, Van Nostrand, New York.

Marx, K. (1976), *Capital*, Volume 1, Penguin, Harmondsworth.

Meisel, H. (1984), 'The pioneers: STC in the Federal Republic of Germany', in MaCoy, R. and Morand, M. (eds.), *Short-Time Compensation: A Formula for Worksharing*, pp. 53–60, Pergamon Press, New York.

Meltz, N. M., Reid, F. and Swartz, G. S. (1981), *Sharing the Work: An Analysis Of the Issues In Worksharing and Job-Sharing*, University of Toronto Press, Toronto.

Menzies, H. (1981), *Women and the Chip: Case Studies of the Effects of Informatics on Employment in Canada*, Institute for Research on Public Policy, Montreal.

Metcalf, D. (1982), *Alternatives to Unemployment*, report No. 610, Policy Studies Institute, London.

Minkler, M. (1981), 'Research on the health effects of retirement: an uncertain legacy', *Journal of Health and Social Behaviour*, Vol. 22, pp. 117–30.

Montgomery, C. (1982), 'Work-sharing plan not success for all firms, sample says', *The Globe and Mail* (Canada), 27/8/82, p. 8.

Mott, P. E., Mann, F. C., McLoughlin, Q. and Warwick, D. (1965), *Shiftwork: Social, Psychological and Physical Consequences*, University of Michigan Press, Ann Arbor.

NBPI (National Board for Prices and Incomes) (1970a), *Hours of Work, Overtime and Shiftworking*, Report No. 161, Cmnd 4554, HMSO, London.

—— (1970b), *Hours of Work, Overtime and Shiftworking*, Report No. 161 (Supplement), HMSO, London.

Nemirow, M. (1984), 'Short-time compensation: some policy considerations', in MaCoy, R. and Morand, M., *Short-Time Compensation: A Formula for Work-sharing*, pp. 158–82, Pergamon Press, New York.

Nollen, S. D. (ed.) (1982), *New Work Schedules in Practice: Managing Time in a Changing Society*, Van Nostrand, New York.

Nord, W. R. and Costigan, R. (1973), 'Worker adjustment to the four-day week: a longitudinal study', *Journal of Applied Psychology*, Vol. 58, No. 1, pp. 60–66.

Oakley, A. (1974), *The Sociology of Housework*, Martin Robertson, Oxford.

Olmstead, B. (1977), 'Job-sharing — a new way to work', *Personnel Journal*, Vol. 50, No. 2, pp. 78–81.

—— (1983), 'Changing times: the use of reduced worktime options in the United States', *International Labour Review*, Vol. 122, No. 4, pp. 479–92.

OECD (Organisation for Economic Cooperation and Development) (1983), *Employment Outlook*, OECD, Paris.

Orpin, C. (1981), 'Effects of flexible working hours on employee satisfaction and performance: A field experiment', *Journal of Applied Psychology*, Vol. 66, pp. 113–15.

Owen, J. D. (1977), 'Flexitime: some problems and solutions', *Industrial and Labor Relations Review*, Vol. 30, pp. 307–13.

—— (1979), *Working Hours: An Economic Analysis*, D. C. Heath, Lexington, Mass.

Parker, S. (1982), *Work and Retirement*, Allen and Unwin, London.

Pearson, P. (1985), *Twilight Robbery*, Pluto, London.

Phillipson, C. (1982), *Capitalism and the Construction of Old Age*, MacMillan, London.

Pierce, J. L. and Newstrom, J. W. (1983), 'The design of flexible work schedules and employee responses: relationships and process', *Journal of Occupational Behaviour*, Vol. 4, pp. 247–62.

Plowman, R. (ed.) (1977), 'Flexible working hours — some labour relations implications', *Journal of Industrial Relations*, Vol. 19, pp. 307–13.

Poor, R. (ed.) (1972), *4 Days, 40 Hours*, Pan, London.

—— and Steele, J. L. (1972), 'Work and leisure: the reactions of people at 4 day firms', in Poor, R. (ed.), *4 Days, 40 Hours*, pp. 57–78, Pan, London.

Ramsay, H. (1977), 'Cycles of control: worker participation in sociological and historical perspective', *Sociology*, Vol. 11, No. 3, pp. 481–506.

Rapoport, R. and Rapoport, R. N. (eds.) (1978), *Working Couples*, Routledge and Kegan Paul, London.

Rathkey, P. (1984), *Work and the Prisoners of Time: The Case for Work-Sharing*, Work and Society, Brighton, Sussex.

Rees, T. L. and Atkinson, P. (eds.) (1982), *Youth Unemployment and State Intervention*, Routledge and Kegan Paul, London.

Reid, F. (1982), 'UI-assisted worksharing as an alternative to layoffs: the Canadian experience', *Industrial and Labor Relations Review*, Vol. 35, No. 3, pp. 319–29.

—— and Meltz, N. M. (1984), 'Canada's STC: A comparison with the California version', in MaCoy, R. and Morand, M. (eds.), *Short-Time Compensation: A Formula for Worksharing*, pp. 106–19, Pergamon Press, New York.

Reyher, L., Koller, M. and Spitznagel, E. (1980), *Employment Policy Alternatives to Unemployment in the Federal Republic of Germany*, Anglo-German Foundation, London.

Robinson, O. and Wallace, J. (1984), *Part-Time Employment and Sex Discrimination Legislation in Great Britain*, Department of Employment Research Paper No. 43, HMSO, London.

Rogers, J. E. Thorold (1906), *Six Centuries of Work and Wages*, Sonnenschein, London.

Rones, P. L. (1981), 'Response to recession: reduce hours or jobs', *Monthly Labor Review*, Vol. 104, No. 10, pp. 3–11.

Schlozman, K. L. and Verba, S. (1979), *Injury to Insult: Unemployment, Class and Political Response*, Harvard, Cambridge, Mass.

Slichter, S. H., Healy, J. J. and Livernash, R. E. (1960), *The Impact of Collective Bargaining on Management*, Brookings, New York.

Sloane, P. J. (1975), *Changing Patterns of Working Hours*, Department of Employment Manpower Paper No. 13, HMSO, London.

Social Services Committee (1982), *Age of Retirement*, HMSO, London.

Solovyov, L. (1962), 'The reduction of employees' working hours in the Soviet Union', *International Labour Review*, Vol. 86, No. 1, pp. 31–41.

Symons, A. (1978), 'Varied working hours — here to stay?', *Work and People*, Vol. 4, No. 1/2, pp. 5–12.

Syrett, M. (1983), *Employing Job-Sharers, Part-time and Temporary Staff*, Institute of Personnel Management, London.

Tavernier, G. (1978), 'Car workers shift to flexible leisure time', *International Management*, October, pp. 39–40.

Teriet, B. (1977), 'Flexiyear schedules — only a matter of time?', *Monthly Labour Review*, Vol. 100, No. 12, pp. 62–5.

Thiis-Evensen, E. (1958), 'Shiftwork and health', *Industrial Medicine*, Vol. 27, pp. 493–7.

Thompson, E. P. (1967), 'Time, work-discipline and industrial capitalism', *Past and Present*, Vol. 38, pp. 56–97.

TUC (Trades Union Congress) (1981), *Report*, TUC, London.

—— (1983a), *Campaign for Reduced Working Time, Progress Report No. 9*, TUC, London.

—— (1983b), *Campaign for Reduced Working Time, Progress Report No. 10*, TUC, London.

—— (1983c), *Campaign for Reduced Working Time, Progress Report No. 11*, TUC, London.

Trade Union Research Unit (1981), *Working Time in Britain*, Anglo-German Foundation, London.

Vallery-Masson, J., Poitrenaud, J., Burnat, G. and Lion, M. R. (1981), 'Retirement and morbidity: a three-year longitudinal study of a French managerial population', *Age and Ageing*, vol. 10, pp. 271–6.

Vekic, D. (1970), 'Introduction and effects of the 42-hour week in Yugoslavia', *International Labour Review*, Vol. 102, No. 3, pp. 255–75.

Voogd, L. (1978), 'Shift work in the Netherlands', in International Labour Office, *Management of Working Time in Industrialised Countries*, pp. 72–5, ILO, Geneva.

Wade, M. (1973), *Flexible Working Hours in Practice*, Gower, Epping.

Walker, J. (1970), 'A review of the literature on the human problems of shiftwork', in NBPI, *Hours of Work, Overtime and Shiftworking*, pp. 76–91, Report No. 161 (Supplement), HMSO, London.

Webb, S. and Cox, H. (1891), *The Eight Hours Day*, Scott, London.

—— and Webb, B. (1902), *Industrial Democracy*, Longman, London.

White, M. (1980), *Shorter Working Time*, Report No. 589, Policy Studies Institute, London.

—— (1981), *Case Studies of Shorter Working Time*, Report No. 597, Policy Studies Institute, London.

—— (1982), *Shorter Hours Through National Industry Agreements*, Department of Employment Research Paper No. 38, HMSO, London.

—— and Ghobadian, A. (1984), *Shorter Working Hours in Practice*, Report No. 631, Policy Studies Institute, London.

Whybrew, E. G. (1964), 'Overtime and the reduction of the working week: a comparison of British and Dutch experience', *British Journal of Industrial Relations*, Vol. 2, No. 2, pp. 149–64.

—— (1968), *Overtime Working in Britain*, Research Paper 9, Royal Commission on Trade Unions and Employers' Associations, HMSO, London.

Wilkinson, R. T. (1978), 'Hours of work and the twenty-four-hour cycle of rest and activity', in Warr, P. B. (ed.), *Psychology at Work*, pp. 17–40, Penguin, Harmondsworth.

Winnett, R. A. and Neale, M. S. (1981), 'Flexible work schedules and family time allocation: assessment of a system change on individual behaviour using self-report logs', *Journal of Applied Behaviour Analysis*, Vol. 14, No. 1, pp. 39–46.

Yoshio, K. (1980), 'The future of the fixed-age retirement system', in Nishikawa, S. (ed.), *The Labor Market in Japan*, pp. 104–23, University of Tokyo Press, Tokyo.

INDEX

Author Index

Aagard, A. K. 140
Allen, R. 37
Allenspach, H. 127, 131
Arkin, W. 115, 116
Arthurs, A. 145
Atkinson, P. 12

Balch, B. W. 140
Beasley, M. 108
Bednaznik, R. W. 97, 98
Bell, R. L. 136
Belous, R. S. 95
Benjamin, B. 163
Benson, J. 119
Best, F. 41, 42, 92, 95, 98
Bienefeld, M. A. 16, 17, 18, 22, 78, 137
Blandy, A. 130, 143
Blyton, P. 3, 36, 39, 159, 160
Bohen, H. H. 127, 128, 131, 133, 134
Bolle, M. 30
Bosworth, D. L. 51, 62, 64, 65, 66, 67, 73
Bourner, T. 62, 64
Boxx, W. R. 139
Boyle, A. 120
Bradlaugh, C. 28
Brittan, S. 36
Brown, S. C. 42, 106, 108
Bruche, G. 72, 150, 158, 159, 162
Burgess, K. 19, 51

Calvasina, E. J. 139
Carpentier, J. 67, 68, 69, 70
Casey, B. 72, 150, 158, 159, 162
Cavendish, R. 12
Cazamian, P. 67, 68, 69, 70
CBI 4, 39, 40, 50, 157
Chiplin, B. 123
Clark, G. 6, 102, 103, 113
Clegg, H. A. 27
Clutterbuck, D. 131
Cook, J. D. 170
Cooper, C. L. 156
Costigan, R. 139, 140, 141

Cox, H. 21
Crona, G. 159, 161
Crouter, A. C. 132
Cuvillier, R. 58

Danish Ministry of Labour 153
Dawkin, P. J. 51, 62, 64, 65, 67, 73
Department of Employment 4, 23, 24, 25, 37, 52, 79, 88, 91, 93, 103, 105, 154, 155
Deuterman, W. V. 106, 108
Dex, S. 6, 103, 106
Dickson, P. 85, 86, 137
Dobrofsky, L. R. 115, 116
Doering, M. 153, 163
Dunham, R. B. 140

Ehrenberg, R. G. 53, 75
Equal Opportunities Commission 110, 111, 119, 120, 121
ETUI 26, 27, 33, 38, 53, 54, 63, 67, 71, 77, 80, 81, 83, 148, 149
European Industrial Relations Review 44
Evans, A. A. 18, 25, 26, 30, 31, 48, 77, 78, 80

Finn, P. 63
Fitzgibbon, G. 128
Fogarty, M. P. 152, 162
Fottler, M. D. 140
Frost, P. 62, 64
Fudge, C. 63, 66

Ghobadian, A. 45, 46
Gibbins, H. de B. 20
Ginneken, W. van 37, 44
Glucklich, P. 109
GMWU 71
Goldberg, A. I. 42, 58
Goodale, J. G. 140
Goodhart, P. 120
Gorz, A. 168
Grais, B. 100
Gutek, B. A. 132

180

Subject Index